BOOK

CATALOGUE

2008

Red Jordan Arobateau

BOOK CATALOGUE
2008 Red Jordan Arobateau
Copyright c. 2007, by Red Jordan Arobateau.

Cover painting, LA SUENA
RED JORDAN AROBATEAU   American (1943-)
La Suena circa 1969. Oil on Canvas 20" x 21".
Artists Collection, San Francisco

Authors photo by Dr. Sam

ISBN: 978-0-6151-7308-5

Published by RED JORDAN PRESS
484 Lake Park Ave. PMB 228
Oakland, CA 94610
USA

A complete literary catalogue of 80-titles by Red Jordan Arobateau according to the author, including all novels, short story & poetry collections, journals, & dramatic plays. Beginning in section one with 'alphabetical' title list. Following, in section two, each title, containing its commentary.

Every title can be ordered online; amazon.com, lulu.com, redjordanarobateau.com & other new & used book internet sites. They can be ordered thru your local bookstore chain, and are carried in selected independent stores. Or buy directly from RED JORDAN PRESS, 484 Lake Park Ave. PMB #228, Oakland, CA, 94610, USA. No prices are included. Prices are subject to change. Go online for current information.

SECTION ONE
List Of Titles

A.

ALEXANDER D'ORO A COLLECTION OF STORIES
THE AGE OF OM -- poetry
ASHCAN BETTY—old collection
ACTS AGAINST THE POWERS OF AUTHORITY--novel
AUTUMN CHANGES (My Unofficial Semi-Autobiography)

B.

THE BACCHANALIAS SOCIETY BASH-- old collection
THE BARS ACROSS HEAVEN--novel
THE BIG CHANGE--novel
THE BLACK BIKER --dike biker series
A BLAX MAN IS NOT A WINDUP DOLL-- old collection
BOOGIE NIGHTS/PARTY LIGHTS-- old collection
THE BLOOD OF CHRIST AGAINST THE LIES OF BABYLON—
-----old collection
BOY CENTER—old collection
BOY'S NIGHT OUT—short stories
BARRIO BLUES-- old collection

C.

COME WITH ME LUCY— novel
CAN'T GO ON ANOTHER DAY --old collection
THE CLUBFOOT BALLERINA/THE PRIMA DONA-- old collection
CARNIVALLA --a play
CHINA GIRL--novel
COMPASSION—my journal

D.

DAUGHTERS OF COURAGE--novel
DAUGHTERS OF COURAGE – a play
DOING IT FOR THE MISTRESS (Gay, Lesbian, Bisexual, Transsexual F*ck
Stories Vol. 3.)
DIRTY PICTURES--novel

4

E.

ELECTRO SHOCK DOKTOR-- old collection
EMPIRE! — novel

F.

FLASH! ON THE HUSTLER --novel
FISHERPEOPLE--novel
FLEAMARKET MOLLY-- old collection
FOR WANT OF THE HORSE THE RIDER WAS LOST--novel

G.

THE GREAT HEART BANK ROBBERY--novel
GARBAGE CAN SALLY-- old collection

H.

HIGHER GROUND--play
HOBO SEX--novel
HOW'S MARS? --novel
A HILLBILLY GIRL IS LIKE A BUTTERFLY --old collection
HOW DON JUAN DIED --a play
HO STROLL—epic novel

I.

THE IRON WOMAN-- poetry
INHABITANTS OF A GHETTOIZED POPULATION --a play

J.

JAILHOUSE STUD--novel
JOURNEY-My Journal

L.

LUCY & MICKEY--novel
LAY LADY LAY--novel
LEADER OF THE PACK dike biker series
LAUGHTER OF THE WITCH -- poetry
THE LOVE LAMENT OF PETER PAIN—old collection
LIGHT AT DAWN-- old collection
LAMENTATIONS IN THE COOL OF THE EVENING—A Journal
LADIES' AUXILIARY OF THE LEFT/CHAMPAGNE, FIRECRACKERS,
GUNSHOTS & THE SMOKE FROM THE DEATH FACTORY: My Diary
1967-1977

LAVANDARETTE OF MY SOLITUDE --a play
THE LOVE LAMENT OF PETER PAIN --a play

M.

IN THE MAELSTROM –a play
TO THE MAN WITH HIS HAT IN HIS HAND ---
-WITH LOVE--   old collection
THE MAN FROM THE BLAX GALAXY-- old collection
MAN GONE/STARVAX— novel
Red Jordan Arobateau's THE MAIDS --a play

N.

THE NEARNESS OF YOU/SORROW OF THE MADONNA—novel

O.

OUTLAWS! -- dike biker series
OUR DYKE HOUSE –a play

P.

PRISONER OF HEARTS—old collection
PASSAGE—My Journal

R.

THE RICH/THE POOR IN SPIRIT—old collection
ROUGH TRADE—short stories

S.

STREET OF DREAMS (Gay, Lesbian, Bisexual, Transsexual F*ck Stories Vol. I & 2)
STORIES FROM THE DANCE OF LIFE, VOL. 1
STORIES FROM THE DANCE OF LIFE, VOL. 2.
STORIES FROM THE DANCE OF LIFE, VOL. 3
SUZIE-Q: A COLLECTION OF STORIES
IN THE STRANGE EMBRACE OF A PRODIGAL-novel
SATAN'S BEST -- dike biker series
STAGE DOOR—epic novel
STREET FIGHTER—novel

T.

TRANNY BIKER --dike biker series

V.

VENGEANCE! --novel

W.

FOR WANT OF THE HORSE THE RIDER WAS LOST--novel
WESTPOINT OF THE UNIVERSE—old collection
WHITE GIRL--old collection
WHERE THE WORD IS NO--novel

Note: old collection indicates that book is part of Red's Re-Photocopy Series. Making available older works ('Ancient Books' as referred to at RED JORDAN PRESS) written pre--1980. Many of them are considered to be amateur writing, thus never forwarded into his main catalogue. In numbers reduced down to 1 or 2 copies each they were sitting in boxes unavailable to collectors, slowly passing into oblivion. This is their resurrection. **No attempt has been made to revise or edit their text; they are reproduced exactly as-is.** Some Ancient books in his catalogue were continued on thru the years—IE., Bars Across Heaven, Ho Stroll, Jailhouse Stud, short story collections Suzie Q. &Alexander D'Oro --Others resurrected; edited and retyped into computer in the 2004 Lulu series: (Vengeance! & Fisherpeople). Titles in this Re-Photocopy Series are from a pool of leftover works, some written as early as the 1960's. They are more expensive, requiring a different processing.

All Red's books must be ordered on a 'as is' basis; many of them are from older stock; & hand made.

Some descriptions may reference an edition of a title, which is now out of print! The current available edition may not contain extraneous material (photos, etc.) as described in this catalogue!

SECTION TWO
Titles & Description

Book reports provided by RED JORDAN PRESS, authors quotes & and other sources as noted.

A.

ACTS AGAINST THE POWERS OF AUTHORITY:
Science Fiction novel. 3rd in a trilogy which is also are the first books in the
author's Unity Of Utopia series.
This Sci-Fi/Futurist novel is third in the trilogy about the Unity of Utopia, but
the series will continue! Acts Against The Powers Of Authority is a wrap-up of
books one (EMPIRE!) and two (Man Gone/Starvax). It has advanced in time to
the year 2097, some 40 years after the other two books; we discover what has
happened to the Unity Of Utopia, and all our heros and beloved characters of
the earlier novels. This book stands alone in reading, you don't have to have
read the other two first, but it helps. This book has politics and adventure and
sex. Some citizens of the Unity of Utopia have broken away from the
dictatorship and started a new world in Africa. Outerspace exploration
continues off of Triton! Read on for this fascinating series!

ALEXANDER D'ORO: A COLLECTION OF STORIES:
Like it's companion anthology SUZIE Q & OTHER STORIES, ALEXANDER
D'ORO contains 5 shorter gems, including the title piece, which is semi
autobiographical and mostly about a fabulous character we first met in Red
Jordan's FLASH! ON THE HUSTLER! Alexander D'Oro-- later, Soltar
Saturn-- a beautiful black sissy, failed theatrical actor, and hustler
extraordinaire. At 35 chapters this piece takes up fully half the book-- and
that's a good thing, for the reader doesn't want it to end! And probably won't
put it down until they've sped through the fast moving developments-- the
growing up of two gay teenagers in which the author, under a pseudonym,
describes his own early years--- and his friend, whose birth name is Bobby
Goldberg. Their victories: "This is the kind of people we were. While the rest
of the students moped along talking about sex, and who got pregnant and had
to drop out of school, we were talking about ideas and the civil rights
movement. All us oddballs." -- And, their downfalls: "Every day for a few
weeks on the way home from school, Bobby was waylaid by a gang of youths
who beat him, socking him in the face and stomach. They rubbed snow in his
face. Blood dripped on the snow, speckling it red. He bent over trying to
protect himself with this hands while they punched him. His mouth was a
bloody mess. He didn't try to fight back--maybe afraid of being killed." --
More about Bobbie: (Who renames himself Alexander, and finally, Soltar.)
"He liked to meet people and was very flexible in his associates. His turf was as
wide as the four corners of the world. While most sissies lived and died on
Chicago's South side."--- "Bobbie confided his own sex life. The days of his
innocence had lasted up until about age 10 when he'd (been approached by) an
old man who had an apartment in the same building they'd lived in down on
40th street. In exchange the man had given Bobby money for soda pop and
candy and little toys." Later: "At the moviehouse in Chicago's' Loop noted for
homosexuality-- and rumored to have lesbians-- Bobby met a rich white man, a
homosexual, a doctor, a john. We will call him John, but that is not his real
name. Bobby was 15; John, 29. They rode around in the doctor's car. The

doctor gave him money, but respected him, or was he cautious of the law, or was it both? they waited to have sex until Bobby turned 16." It is this 'john' whom Bobby/Alexander later will blackmail for fabulous sums.

Next comes THE INVESTIGATOR; opening with a scene of 2 African American dikes having a discussion in the femmes living room: "Etta's ex-husband had told the authorities she was a lesbian because he wanted custody of their children: two daughters. He had taken her to court. This was a dirty, underhanded blow." For the simple reason, back in those days being a lesbian was seen as a bad influence. An Investigator from the Department of Social Services begins visiting unexpectedly, any time of day, asking all kinds of questions, to evaluate the children's home life. So Etta must keep up the pretense of not being gay, for 8 long weeks before the court date. The deception Etta must undergo is told with humor: "Miss Dandley showed up looking harder then Alexis (Etta's roommate) was. Had on three-piece blue suit, no makeup... "She comes in here in her suits, her hair is short. She looks like a damn bulldyke her own damn self." A slip up occurs: "And then Alexis's calmly informs me one day, of the cast on my leg--everybody had signed it." She pointed to the white cast with her finger. By now the blue ink had been washed away. "It had 'Bev & Carole' on it in a big red heart. And 'Mable and Joan Forever.' Alexis asked me, 'Have you thought about your cast?' Here I was on this very couch sitting up here all in Miss Dandley's face with the cast and saying, "Aw, I'm not gay." Etta laughed, her eyes twinkled. She moaned both in laughter and pain."

ALEXANDER D'ORO is mostly a black-of-center collection, with the exception of HARBOR LIGHTS, and, another of Red Jordan's tales about a very special person, which comes next; THE CHRISTIAN MISSIONARY OF THE BARS. (There are about 4 of these tales, scattered throughout his Shorter Work Anthologies.) It's the usual format.... Stormy, an Irish dike with red/golden hair is holding court in the gay tavern with her associates; this evening, African American Monk, & Stormy's wild girlfriend Donetta, et al. "The night passed with its gaiety, which was often a mask people wore, being unreal." They talk of Spirit. Of their immediate problems, their lives olives, dreams and desires.

HARBOR LIGHTS. A portrait of an introverted lonely young woman who rides the commute train back and forth for companionship. "Why didn't she talk? Why didn't she join a woman's support group? Why didn't she have a lover? Why was she the way she was? What was she waiting for? She was as the lake in winter, it's ice frozen over."

HOT SAUCE the final story in the collection. In it reappear 2 characters, Prince & Flip the reader will recognize from STORIES FROM THE DANCE OF LIFE, HO STROLL, & BARS ACROSS HEAVEN. Prince, a high yella butch, is quite a player, while poor Flip, older, hard working & richer is often alone. Flip finally meets a young fast lady. --The first inkling of problems to come is when we discover the ladies name; HOT SAUCE. And she lives up to the reputation! In Flips recounting to Prince of a party, Hot Sauce shows out: "THIS PARTY'S SUPPOSE TO BE FO' WOMEN! THE MINUTE I GET HERE A BIG UGLY NIGGER PUTS HIS HANDS ON ME, ASKING DO I HAVE A CIGARETTE, TRYING TO HUSTLE ME! GET AWAY FROM

ME NIGGERS I'M GAY I'M A DIKE! YOU CANT DOMINATE ME! YOU KAIN'T DO NUTHIN FO' ME!" Via telephone, Prince & Flip discuss the previous evening: "Hot Sauce showed out at the party." The yellow butch told Prince in amusement. "Yeah? Wadda she do? Take her clothes off? You always seem to know those type... So do I. We attract 'em." Prince said, mildly interested."

As usual, humor mixed with biting truth; analysis of the human soul, interlaced by great dialogue. Another offering of Master Artist Red Jordan Arobateau.

Book Review provided by RED JORDAN PRESS 2005.

THE AGE OF OM:

Poetry Collection. This is the first half of the approximately 800 poems written by the author over a twenty-year time frame. The second half is THE IRON WOMAN. There is also a poetry sampler; LAUGHTER OF THE WITCH. First of Red Jordan's 2-volume poetry collection. Same format as THE IRON WOMAN. AGE OF OM's table of contents lists: Early Poems (1957-1967). Sex & Romance, Short Poems & Valentines. Women's Liberation (1970's). Blues. Epic Poems. God Poems & Other Later Works (1976-1978). The contents of volume I. differs from II with the Valentines, a format the author invented, and the inclusion of the Sex & Romance category. This novel contains two of Red's most amazing Epic Poems; COME TO THE BLACK MARKET, and THE CITY WHERE THERE'S FIRE! Also, an early work, HERALDS OF THE RESURRECTION. We quote below: "Come to the Black Market. World metropolis. Ambassadors, dignitaries talk
in continental accents.
Austere figures
examine merchandise.
--Capricorn's of thoughts. Fabric
of illusions.
Dust of foreign aromas. Here are cosmic heads who represent
all elements! Dreamers, liars.
Weary people
draining soil out of their fingertips. One hustler
distorted by her strange clothes,
reveals her soul thru a scowl. "I GOT FIRE!" She's one of you.
She balances her scale to the universe. Come to the Black market.
--And you will be yourself." HERALDS OF THE RESURRECTION: "I am
Colored
as New Orleans once cradled
with its eyes on the white world
privilege,
nursing its fantasies.
A Goblin Girl
The street lamps shed.
Yellow, hair a-curl.
I un-fold out of limbo.
Out of the crook of a magicians sleeve!

I grew,
PRESTO!
A Bulldagger!

Pimped--down in fine clothes,
mocking The Man.
Closed up in my coat.
A flamboyant stud.
Into my armsleeves
flickers my vagrant form,
into a pout.
And my head is a vapor beneath
a Harlem Tweed.
--Into a cloth child
by these streets,
dreamed.

An improvisation from Scorpio.
A trombone slash.
A cymbal slide
born upward for a jag.
I'm a dancer! A
molecule of light!

This
air-shattered cry!

ME!"   Book Review provided by RED JORDAN PRESS, 2005

ASHCAN BETTY:
Old collection. Guess I should call these books of the Re-Xerox program The
Juvenilia Series—even tho I was in my mid-30's when writing most of them.
Why they are predominately lesser then a few done around the same time such
as BARRIO BLUES, or THE RICH/THE POOR IN SPIRIT, I can't account
for. Why they aren't the caliber of say HOWS MARS? Or, FOR WANT OF
THE HORSE THE RIDER WAS LOST, both written even earlier in my
career, is just fate. My supposition is they weren't ignited by events
transpiring in my life. I didn't put as much of my heart into them. They are
more concoctions then original intense stuff drawn directly from the
wellsprings of my daily events, desires, and feelings. But I just had to write
something! I took copious notes as part of daily work as an author,
accumulating different studies on a variety of topics over months to write many
of these books. After numerous planned treks to San Francisco's Chinatown,
during the late 1970's notes for CHINA GIRL were taken but sat unused until
returning to them in 2005 creating the masterpiece of the same name —while
giving it a transsexual theme. 1978-'79 near the end of an extravagant
vacation—not worrying for 1 year about money-- in which I pumped out all

this writing, I did THE SCAVENGER TRILOGY. Consisting of 3 novels, FLEAMARKET MOLLY December 1978, the longer GARBAGE CAN SALLY April 1979, and ASHCAN BETTY in February 1980. During that time frame discovered I was about to be very very poor. Dad's money had run out, the mortgage paid in advance was going to come due, plus having just renounced a brief, lucrative marijuana-growing business for the sake of Jesus and my new Christianity, I became desperate and began recycling garbage, while entering back into the job market as an Aid to disabled people. All the notes from this trilogy are first hand accounts. That was really me at the fleamarket, and picking up sacks of garbage & going thru them at the side of the road!

AUTUMN CHANGES: (My Unofficial Semi Autobiography), Part Four: Chances are you've never heard of Red Jordan Arobateau. He was only brought to my attention recently when I was assigned to review his book and found an interview by indie-acclaimed author Michelle Tea for a local, weekly newspaper. I was fairly apprehensive of this "unofficial semi-autobiography, part four," as other autobiographies I have read recently-- John Stuart Mill, the early progenitor of utilitarianism, and Akira Kurosawa, the world famous Japanese film director-- finish at a mere 197 and 189 pages respectively. My fears were not assuaged, as the first chapter or section was very self-centered-- even more then your average autobiography-- as Red describes his irritation and distaste for the local queer cognoscenti's lack of acceptance of his genius works of art, written and visual. His sustenance is the knowledge that some day people will know his name and he'll be handsomely rewarded. To me, self-described "misunderstood genius" often translates to "crazy-nut-job."
The book's tone, however, quickly changes as Red continues on to tell the impressive story of his five-year transition from woman to man and his amazing life. AUTUMN CHANGES is figuratively an unorthodox fairytale, philosophically a manifesto, and literally, "a testimony of his first transition years intermixed with remembrances of things past."
The book follows Red as he is separated from a loving father to live with an unfortunately mentally ill mother, a victim of abuse and "blind" grandmother. As a young queer artist, he visits the seedy local Chicago blues and jazz venues and prohibited queer bars, searching for a girlfriend or someone to spend the night with, then moves to San Francisco's infamous Tenderloin district. The stories, however are not chronologically presented, and instead swiftly jump between the young and younger Red, and later, to a more present-day, transitioning Red. This happens in quick, fluid motions that take on an almost surreal feel reminiscent of Margaret Atwood, and oddly, Louis F. Celine.
We all have many different sets of glasses through which we view and interpret the world that surrounds us, and what struck me as particularly interesting here was the multitude of perspectives that Red deftly writes from: as both a man and a woman feeling that he was a man in a woman's body since he was a young boy; as a queer activist and a political activist, protesting the Vietnam war and the US. Army's more recent excursions; as a transsexual activist and counselor; and as a heartbroken lover. These experiences among others in Red's 60-plus years, leave the reader with rich and diverse stores.

Stylistically and aesthetically, the book is very DIY, with red type, edits, and-- as you may have guessed-- it is self-released. The book is printed on thin paper with slightly ticker covers and typed without many corrections. Red writes in a stream-of-consciousness with a reckless lack of concern for corrections, spelling, grammar, etc. To Red, this is art in its purest form:

> His writings unedited, misspelled (sic) and since
> they are done by the oldfashion (sic) typewriter
> method, and not computer, can't be spellchecked
> (sic) in cyberspace.. So the buyer is getting a blast
> from the original motherlode (sic). Fresh.
> Unadulterated. Non-tampered by lacky (sic) proof-
> readers, fresh-faced typest (sic) keying their way
> thru (sic) college, who don't understand the differ-
> ence between black vernaculars 'fonky' and the ofey
> 'funky'-- thus insist on revising his pure stream of
> conscious with their abrupt seemingly-harmless
> 'corrections' (sic) which are in fact corruption's.
> (Page. 1220).

While this relaxed usage of language and such was confusing at times -- I have an idea but I'm not positive what "clitdechtomy" is -- it was not much of a deterrent, as the words flowed well along the pages.
Overall, this book is an important read for all; particularly those of us who lack knowledge of the "trans" community, along with those who are involved in said community. As a straight, white male, I found the book extremely interesting. For people in the trans community, the book might act as a resource. Essentially, the book is informative in that it documents the highs and lows of life during the transition; friends who'll ignore or back away from their friendship with you; loved ones who turn their backs on you; excitement from passing for the gender you wish to be; the complications of changing the gender on your driver's license; the continuous injections of "T" (or "E", whatever your fancy might be); being outed by one's doctor; ect. The book left me wanting to read more and learn more about Red and his transition. While four volumes may seem a bit much, I'm sure Red has enough juice, enough passion and enough stories to fill those and many other pages, and keep it fascinating and worth the time to read. -- Vince Larussa
Book Review by Vince Larussa for MAXIMUM ROCK N ROLL, March 2005

AUTUMN CHANGES (My Unofficial Semi-Autobiography.):
Published in 5 volumes, (aprox 1,400 pages). This volume is almost at the end of The Work, which is sold in 5 separate parts or in its entirety. Typewritten in the authors original font and not spell checked. Some marvelously funny episodes, an adequate amount of sex scencs, illicit sex clubs, dominatrix, drag queens, & all kinds of case situations of other trans people, are illustrated in this information packed book. AUTUMN CHANGES is first and foremost an art book about FTM's (and MTF's) and all other kinfolk on the gender spectrum including those who transition back and forth from one end to the other! This is not merely fiction, it's history. We must mention AUTUMN

CHANGES quotes everybody; Red's own classic lines from different volumes of his prose & poetry--and other authors; from Kathy Acker to President Ronald Ragen. The Bible. And Djuna Barnes.

This book is so engrossing, it must read, read & read! If one part doesn't get to you pick it up and begin somewhere else!

Excerpts of this epic work have appeared in the FTMI Newsletter. this is the opening volume of RJA's life work, his Unofficial Semi-Autobiography; 1,600 pages long, which has been divided into 5 parts for publishing purposes in the underground RED JORDAN PRESS. Each volume is sold individually or the whole set together. This book in its original typewritten font, unspellchecked, is a collectors dream! AUTUMN CHANGES begins with 2 short introductory pieces. TALES OF TRANSMAN Parts 1 & 2, where we encounter the 5 year old Red in his family home on the South Side of Chicago. Scenes switch fast up to 1998, still female bodied, then jumps back to 1948, to depict more of Red's history as a boy/girl; a mixed raced tomboy, that defines his childhood in the colored ghetto of Chicago's South Side. Glimpses of this early crossdresser (age 7), playing baseball outdoors in the alley with other boys, or inside with chemistry, and erector sets & refusing to play with dolls. Becoming aware of his sexuality later in teenage, by reading pulp novels such as Journey to a Woman, and Ann Bannon's Bebo Brinker series. In some instances AUTUMN CHANGES resembles the whole regular shebang of trans auto biographies -- except this one is different----Transman is an artist, a spiritual searcher, & a sexual libertine. Arobateau's style is to flash back & forth in his memories rather then a typical linear progression. A different date annotates the subsequent paragraph, and locates the reader immediate in time: □□1972 Transman purchases a kingsized bed.--Visualizing many hot naked females in it. Does not realize it will be nearly 15 solid years of more aloneness interspersed by 4 or 5 aborted relationships and a dozen 20-minute hookers, until he meets his wife. AUTUMN CHANGES is a bookfull of procedural information about FTM's & MTF's as well; something most trans books (fiction/autobiographies) don't have. Usually being about either one or the other; although the majority of it is about the men: It is August 1998. 3 weeks away from top surgery. 2 months until his first hormone shot. A picture of the guys assembled at a support group: One handsome stocky male--with a totally flat chest leads the group. A greater butch then the others, he observes. Jealously wells up in Transman. This is how he longs to look! Without hormone shots he never will. This book's snapshots flash back and forth. Red Jordan Arobateau, teenager. Young adult in his 20's. And middle age. How change hurts his wife of 16 years--the lovely Jasmine: How do you really think I'm going to react to this sex change? Says the wife at last, wearily.... I haven't thought about it really. Confesses Transman. He's so tired. It is the era of the transgender clinic. We see the Famous Tom Waddell facility in which we get a view of flamboyant colorful girls as well as the boys: At the time the doctors thought it would serve exclusively male to female sex workers who lived in the Tenderloin. Now it sees trannys coming from all over. Arobateau packs so much information into this amazing book; medical, surgical procedures for both MTF's and FTM's; race, class, spirituality, & plots; huge amounts of dialogue which are often funny; confessions during support groups. He shows

14

how important transition is to the true transsexual: It is of vital importance to be masculine. To uphold his manhood.--Even while still inside a girl body. Womanizing kinds of things tear down his/her ego, and her maleness. The best intentioned shopclerks who recognize a woman under his mashed down cap, and address him politely as 'Mam' after scrutiny, doing their best to be polite; the large men who step aside and let him go through a door first--is it his age-- or his perceived gender? It's too feminizing. He would go back to using drugs. Drink himself to death. Other men in the groups testify how close to suicide they were--and that transition was the only escape. Through these random journals l

Excerpts (from chapters) from AUTUMN CHANGES: The Unofficial Semi-Autobiography of Red Jordan Arobateau:
1.
1998.
The sky is slate gray in the eastern sky, and in need of a storm.
Transman stands,--5'3". 160 pounds. Masculine attire; slacks, jacket, on a square body. His shoulders thick from previous years of weight training. Stomach flat.
There is a storm within his/her soul. He is on the borderline of decision.
2.
1948.
Transboy is age 5. 3' tall. 50 pounds. Wears a purple & orange teeshirt over his flat little child chest; bluejeans and sneakers.
He plays with toy soldiers, miniature trucks. Has an Erector set with which he creates metal buildings; and a chemistry set containing Bunsen burner, testubes & vials. And disdains his girl toys.-- A doll and carriage sit idle, dusty, in the living room of their material-comfortable middleclass home-- never even having been moved to either Transboys bedroom, nor to his/her playroom.
3.
During my childhood in the late 1940's, I actually thought for an interval of time I had to become a boy or I would die.-- "God turn me into a boy." Was my ongoing prepubescent prayer. And I can't remember how old I was, 7 or 8 maybe. Psychiatrists suggest it's typical of abused children to forget their childhood. I had a bad, abused childhood at the hands of my mother, and have blocked out lot-- but I remember it was my constant daily and nightly mantra at that time-- that I must grow a penis between my legs miraculously.
Instantly. Must wake up one morning having been changed into a boy. And anger, so great inside that my heart wanted to burst out of my chest and my throat turned dry.
In the 1940's in Chicago Illinois, there was no visible queer movement. The army-to-come was still composed of foot soldiers scattered here and there across the broad planesland of America. In any African American community, or white, you could see visible gays/transgenders sprouting up between the normal school children like strange new vegetables in a garden.
I was born into a black bourgeoisie family of very lightskinned people. My mother and her parents of African descent, and my father of a different

nationality, South of the Border, Latin. Racism surrounded us. Another unpleasant picture.

Girls in my neighborhood on the South Side worked hard at housework; were forced to help their mothers. My best friend, playmate Diane, was given an incredible workload. We were age ten.

Diane did her families ironing. Laundry. And scrubbed the kitchen floor on her knees. I didn't have to do any of this because of my mother's mental illness incapacitating her from standing guard over me. In fact my father did all the cooking, washed dishes, sent out dirty clothes out to a laundry that washed, ironed, folded & bundled it; and once per week a maid came in to dust & vacuum.

Definitely I was not a woman. I'd never fit that description. Female-- yes, because that's the biological body to which I was born. And have been living in this state all my life.

When I first realized I was lesbian;--that is, me, being encased in my female body lusting for other females-- which made me by scientific definition, a lesbian-- that instantly became my great, all consuming focus.-- To have sex with women.-- That, and being an artist. This seemed to solve any questions in the sex department. I didn't realize it wasn't just sexual preference that was the issue, but gender identification also. Few people were speaking about that in 1957. Christine Jorgensen was going to be the first to break the ice.

4.

In the 1950's it was books like Journey To A Woman, or Odd Girls Out, and Twilight Lovers, read discretely, passed from one tan, yellow, or brown hand to the other, secretively around the kitchen table at my girlfriend Carole's parent's home on the West side of the black ghetto--that showed the misunderstood world of women who love women. This journey to self understanding. Understanding of a sexual preference so confusing in the '50's, which has now become for some of us here in the 1990's, a journey to the man-within. As a butch dike at the FTM/Butch conference says, eloquently, "We're constantly pushing new frontiers."

Back in 1959 we slapped cards down on the kitchen table in cutthroat games of Spades, or poker. Dressed in slacks, mans shirt, boots; short hair; drank beer & gin, or bourbon, a very butch and drunk lesbian, I was becoming an adult.

6.

1967.

Young Transman, age 23, stands beside the window of his flat in a Victorian house. A recent arrival to the city of Saint Francis.-- It is a condemned building.

A pile of men's suit jackets lays over a mattress on the floor which passes as a bed. He/she has just returned from shopping at a thrift store--the Goodwill, across town in the Mission district.

A powerful feeling comes over him.

He has always worn butch clothes but none so severe as these. He has slipped his muscular shoulders into one jacket; a physique fit from working out at karate training & calisthenics since age 15. Whips it back off, in a sudden inspiration, and walks across the painted board floor to a dresser drawer and gets an Ace bandage--relic form a prior karate injury (he often had to bind up his knee or tape his toes) --winds the beige elastic cloth around his chest. In minutes his contour is transformed. Medium-size breasts now flattened into his chest give it the appearance of the buffed chest of a hunky weightlifter in a gym.

Now Transman strides to the mirror again; whips the jacket back on and looks. A near-male image of himself looks back at him from the mirror.

This image ignites a fire between his legs. He begins to strut back and forth across his living room.

I walked the streets in drag off and on for several years; like a deaf mute; not communicating because my high-pitched voice might reveal me to be female. By a rough sign language of my hands pointing at this, or that item behind the counter in a store; or a drink from a bottle in a straight tavern--while waving my money in the air. With a smile on my face I'd raise my hands greeting hello/goodby--all without uttering a word. But occasionally by accident, would emit a low guttural gurgle as I hastily stopped words ready to spill out, dead in my throat.

8.

Transbutch has been in San Francisco about a year. Inspired by a night of love with a young woman which left me feeling something was lacking--that sex organ, a dick, between my legs to fuck her with-- instead of the fingers of my right hand; or me riding her thigh with my clit to get-off myself.

The next day I begin construction on an amazing device--a plaster of Paris dick.

This dildo was constructed of plaster poured over a wire frame. It was huge and heavy.-- Heavy enough to kill somebody if you held it by it's base and hit them on top of their head.

In my hotel room in the Tenderloin, housed between a babbling crone and continuous wino transients, I subsisted on welfare vouchers, a series of part-time minimum wage jobs ($1.75 per hour) and handouts from my dad.

I valiantly pecked away at the manual typewriter by day, writing down adventures I'd had at Mauds Study the night before; and worked on reshaping my plaster of Paris dick. Now attaching an elastic band to secure it to my crotch.

I could roam the Tenderloin streets with a full hard on, flat chest, men's clothes, hat on my head-- and if I didn't talk, and reveal my high voice, nobody would know I'm still a dike.

14.

Transman has breasts. Two big lumps of flesh. Try's to ignore them because he can't afford surgery. -- The bilateral mastectomy.-- Which costs $5,000 at that time. So flattens himself by wearing 3 tight teeshirts. And keeps these teeshirts on faithfully during the sex act.

26.

We 2 spirit people; we're just born this way. This constant disphoria creates a lot of art, a lot of energy, a lot of suicide.

Some call our trangendered journey--finding our true selves.

There are biological explanations for our behavior; scientists theorize this rare condition called Gender Identity Disorder is caused by a misfiring in the

17

development of an infants brain region called the hypothalamus---which controls gender identification and behavior-- while still bathed in the amniotic sea of the womb.

The evidence says that our gender identity is formed biologically, early during brain development and is irreversible.

I have started out my life's journey as a 5 year old tomboy crossdressing in boys clothes.--A child transvestite.

T's stance was always off-center of the lesbian community.-- A boy dike. Never truly an integral part of women's events.

Here remunerated are some of the reasons for his discontent--both past, present & future.

>   Bad service in restaurants.
>   Non hiring for jobs.
>   Dates with bewildered hookers.

Transman is convinced he/she'd be dead by now, had he been a born-male. He still would have had the same broken home, the same abuse, the same life-- conditioning due to the apartheid of his birth neighborhood which was the segregated black/white inner city of 1940's Amerika.

He'd still be a mulatto nigger on the wrong side of the tracks. White enough to be hated by his own people. Black enough to be ostracized by whites.

As a man he might have entered the jail system or got hooked on narcotics, or died in a barroom brawl a lot faster then as a woman.

His ego-manic schemes unfettered as a male might, by now have crashed him into the jagged rocks of society and broken him to bits. As a woman he was well aware of his limits, he was more cautious. Had less allusions. And as a consequence didn't fall as far nor break down completely.

Transman, of African American descent & Latin, including Indian blood, plus white, is actually a mixed race person; for which there is no category in the 1940;s thru to the late 1970's. So he is a technical nobody. His race has never been clear--like the way people want it to be. "Either you're white or you're black! Which one is it!" Society informs him-- thru it's judgmental people, it's census records, it's applications for work, school, loans, rentals et al.

Transman could have died in the race riots of the 1960's.--Beaten to death by other blacks mistaking him for white.

But he has survived. By luck, cunning, cowardice & because of his driving sense of a mission to accomplish--to continue to produce his fine arts paintings-- hence an awareness that he must preserve his life for some greater good, beyond himself.

Planets hang in black space above the building tops.

And the universe whirls by at a great rate of speed.

27.

Around 1992-1994, began to see Transmen sprouting up around San Francisco--shooting T.--Many still with big breasts, unable to afford the costly removal surgery.

4 years later, in 1998, I was to have this operation myself, and begin hormone treatment.

You must be very dedicated to do this transformation, and succeed. Because people will try to stop you in different ways. They will be certain to tell you: "Be sure this is what you want--there's no going back!"

Friends are horrified. "Testosterone is a growth hormone! It increases your metabolism! You're going to age before your time! You're going to be a shriveled up old man at age 60!"

"Testosterone is a violent drug! It'll make you go into wild rages and murder people!"

"You'll be half male and half female!" They exclaim, shocked. Telling lies and half lies.--Which doesn't help him at all.

The doctor, well meaning, who is helpful in other situations says this. Your gay preacher in the queer church says it.

Everyone.

It has a weakening effect.--But the locomotive is already chugging down the track--to freedom.

Thank God!

He was one of that rare race of people who is loyal to the urgings of their soul.
53.

He had to make the telephone call. Such a simple thing, it was difficult to do.--To put his name on a list to begin chemical transition towards the male sex.

How the week flew by! --He didn't have time or space. Too busy cleaning at employers houses--where he dare not make his call.

Finally he gets privacy and space.-- And is glad. Because the nurse puts him on hold; and finally, calls him back-- it takes 2 hours.

But it's done! He has the information of how to proceed thru the redtape and protocol at the clinic.

His appointment is set!

When our early ancestors 60,000 years ago first discovered fire and learned to read the stars, they went out of Africa by torchlight, venturing into new continents.

There is a price.-- You leave behind the old things.

"FREAKS! QUEERS! YOU OUGHT TO DIE! FUCKING QUEERS!"

"Look at that! That... thing... with that woman! What does it think it is? Is it a fag or a lesbian or some kind of freak or what? It's just DISGUSTING!"

The stereotypical queer who lived streetwise, wore men's clothes, dying because he/she is afraid to go to the hospital and have her identity unmasked in a room of jeering healthcare workers & Fascist docktors. "LOOK! IT'S A WOMAN BELOW THE WAIST!"

Transman emerges from under the covers--awake. His mind is black & blue with hate. He's been battered--by memory.

I have to fight for every goddamn thing in my life!

Although Transman is very afraid--he will go thru with these procedures. Now is the time!

There's no turning back!

He wants to go as far as he can. --To the furthest end of masculinazation which for years he has already by dress, manner, performance--and thru every available means--now aided by modern science.

Pushing himself to the limits of his inner man. This inner man which has pushed him from day one. Pushed him into boy jeans and little teeshirts after struggling with his stressed mother morning after morning. Drove him out of doors to play football with neighborhood boys, instead of stay inside with dolls.-- Following this inner path scripted to be male, by genetic code.

The week of the Fall Equinox he began T.-- It was a magical time. Dying ghost of life descending into the earth, so the soil can be made ready for rebirth.

410.

Autumn Changes!

It is with fire, regret, energy, expectations, weariness, that I look back at my life; beginning at that time of transformations--of a dream fulfilled, of this goal (which has been foreshadowed by premonitions inside Jungian dreams) this time of love & lust; now all these memories of it along with my childhood & teens & young adulthood all compounding into each other....

It is like the drowning sailor sinking into the sea for the 3rd time, who sees her entire life pass before her as she sinks under the waves--those stray ends which were not tied up, the paths not taken, the regrettable actions never atoned for. Transformation is dying-- and being reborn again-- as something else. A fact many companions of sex changes can never learn to accept.

1950.

Downwind, Chicago's South Side, smells from the slaughter house-- always in the early afternoon, 1, or 2pm; 'Meat Packer to the World', that odor on the air, a great oily aroma of animals killed for food for America's dinner table. A cow is pushed wild, thrashing screaming wordlessly for it's life down a chute, at the bottom, a huge muscled man with a sledge hammer towers over it and splits its brains open.

My friends today-- 50 years later-- who are Vegans, are to be admired for their love of animals. To stop eating meat would end the pain of countless animals 'forced down the chute'. Transman prays solemnly over his meals. He gives thanks for the flesh of animals devoured. He prays for surcease of all pain. He supports Animal Rights activists to make the meat brokers give cattle full range grazing, instead of being penned in overcrowded stalls. To bring them into the world & let them have happy lives-- before a humane slaughter, at an older age.

Mesquito repellent, which smelled like turpentine. Fireflies. 102 degree heat. Summer. His father takes him to Lake Michigan at dawn so they can cool off in the blue gray water before he goes to work.

Back home, on summer vacation from the Laboratory school, he lays on his makeshift cot set up in his playroom, right by his fathers small mattress dragged out there to catch cool breezes of morning, back on that porch addition at the end of the flat. He is reading The Lives of Bridey Murphy. America's most recent introduction to the concept of reincarnation. He is ten. Past lives... Martians... Science Fiction.... Transchild devours books... He is beginning his art... a desk... pencils... pens... newspaper articles about the KKK clipped from LIFE magazine, enclosed in plastic protectors placed into his notebook. He sits at his desk writing stuff. His colorful paintings from school line the long hallway of their flat...

Remembrance of things past... past lives... illusion so strong as to be convincing of truth? Or reality itself! Mysteries of the universe, still to be unlocked! We are all destined to go down the chute, to the slaughter. We are meat, being devoured by humankind. We are sailors, sinking for the 3rd, final time. Drowning inside an unspeakable world, but having visions and dreaming dreams...
La Fata! El Destino!*
    *-- Fate! Destiny!

THE BACCHANALIAS SOCIETY BASH:
Old collection. Addendum to WESTPOINT OF THE UNIVERSE, this is a separate title, a short sequel. The Grand Irish Heroine amid the wild pack of her phoneroom friends. Her last chapter on earth.

BOY'S NIGHT OUT:
Six Short Stories. This collection of shorter works is done in a neat spell-checked & edited font. Contains the following titles: Cum E-Z, Rubber Room, Boys' Night Out, Poppa, Golden Showers, Oral service. Used as part of the curriculum at UC Berkeley.
An interweave of stories that chronicle gay life and don't pull no punches.
  Published by Red Jordan Press 2001--3rd edition. Copyright 1991. From Cum EZ-Lesbian Cum Stories with Feeling & Meaning Vol. 1-5.

BARRIO BLUES:
Beginning before her first year of age at chapter zero, the story of a Latina Lesbian growing up in el barrio de San Francisco Mission. A look at her family life, sisters, brothers, parents. La escuela, La Iglaise. Each chapter in this marvelous work is a year of Libertads life. Her ambitions. Her life struggle. Her personal growth. The women she takes to bed, and her subsequent adventures. HOT! HOT! Another Masterwork from the pen of Poet/Artist Author Red Jordan Arobateau, Barrio Blues is completely spiced up with some Spanish words, and phrases. A true reading experience!

BARS ACROSS HEAVEN:
This controversial first-published novel of Red Jordan Press, manufactured after Red's poetry chapbooks of the early 1970's, got it's first paid typist, and mass release at the end of that decade and has been a steady seller since. It is an off-shoot of the larger work HO STROLL.
BARS ACROSS HEAVEN-- Red Jordan's blockbuster dike novel first surfaced into the gay literary scene in 1979. It & HO STROLL were both written circa 1974-'75, back to back. When the author, awestruck at the stack of notes piled on his desk for HO STROLL, acquired while a participant in The (Street) Life briefly 2 years before, decided to yank out a bunch of the papers and write a short, quick read which is what BARS ACROSS HEAVEN is. A powerful, brief, glimpse of 2 worlds simultaneously inhabited by one character, an underclass butch dike of color, Flip Jordan. By night on the ho-track hustling scene & criminal underworld, by day the created sanity of a middle class women's therapy group.

The scenes shift rapidly between ordinary gay bar life of those by-gone days, the criminal underground, and the safe, protected environment of the Support Group composed of bourgeoisie professional women, who try to help the antisocial Flip get the things she wants for herself & come to terms with her frustrating life.

The action is fast & raw. Complete with true-rendered dialogue of the street players. The reader boldly bold steps underworld: "First thing that morning Flip had visited the pawnshop; sold four stolen tapedecks, so she could eat. This is how she made her money. Hustling."

Early on we see Flips discomfiture on being a person of mixed race heritage. "A hi-yella African American amid blacks." -- A nigga on the chalk side. And whites of the gay bar, who shun her: "Flip leaned against the wall, tried to appear nonchalant. The bar crowd did it's thing. No one noticed her. She felt like a sore thumb. Her chalk white face in the Afro American sea of blackness. Lone figure, un-movable in this sea of dancing people, who (so she thought) were together in pairs and in the IN CROWD."

A telling scene at a 'segregated' dike baseball game. The hero, Flip sits and simmers under her hat like a pressure cooker, until misplaced anger (problems arising from her bi-racial status) erupt, is well portrayed.

There are scenes of Flip in the street, hanging out in hustlers dives along Oakland's ho stroll amid giant men: "Suddenly, blue and purple flooded Flip's brain. The big giant came up to her. The man towered over her. "Say MAN gimmie a light, BROTHER! WHOOPS! Excuse me Sister! His pool game was over, his stick clattered on the table, where he'd thrown it. "Say, is you a man or a lady?"

Enter another of Arobateau's fabulous characters: "Ruby jitterbugged on tapered legs. She wrapped her coat tight around her shoulders in a gust of wind. --Her lips glistened. A silver smile against her dark skin. Her eyes sparkling with turquoise make-up gave her a diamond effect. But this beautiful woman went right on and lied her lies." It's Ruby from Red Jordan's beautiful crafted pimp-ho novella HOW RUBY GOT THERE. (Found in the collection STORIES FROM THE DANCE OF LIFE VOL. 3.)

Then come the scenes which made BARS ACROSS HEAVEN additionally controversial within 1970's lesbian literature; seeing Flip & a black prostitute in bed together in a sexually explicate scenario of play-for-pay: "Ruby had taken Flip for a trick many times. This older woman had become one of her regulars. She came down to the stroll to date some girl every few weeks or so. Ruby thought as she walked down to the club what was in store for her."---
"Ruby looked around in the dim light, then she saw the bulldagger. She was very glad to see the familiar hawklike face under its blue hat. Ruby grinned and walked over."

The reader will be amazed at the contrast of low-down street, & barroom scenes interspersed with middle class group 'therapy sessions.' Lacing these two worlds together is great dialogue, an evolving plot, and the most insightful intimate revelations of character as one witnesses the transformation of Flip, due to the care she receives at the Women's Group.

The reader will truly want to make this first class book part of their collection; listen while Flip speaks: "I was now listening to her soul. I had touched

something real. That love they had given me was beyond the surface of appearances. After the meeting, as the sisters swirled around, a pregnant woman came up to me. She said, "I just wanted to tell you, I think you're a very brave woman!" Flip sputtered. Tears broke. She stood in her tennis shoes, wrinkled blue denim shirt. She held her wide-brim hat with its red-checked rag in her hand."
Book Review provided by RED JORDAN PRESS, 2005.

THE BIG CHANGE:
This is a copy of the original book (written in the early 1960's) with its original miss-spelling & typos intact! A collectors item! The tale of a mtf transsexual. (Male to female.) The attitudes and viewpoints of transsexuals of that era-- before Stonewall, when the Harry Benjamin Standards of Care ruled supreme. A young boys tale as a cross-dressing prostitute on drugs stumbling thru the streets of Chicago's queer district, thru her later transition to a triumphant female showgirl.
Published by Red Jordan Press--second printing, 1996. Copyright 1976. When we first visit Sandy-Paul, Arobateau's middle America proto-type transsexual, she is in male 'drab'. Quite a poor ragged boy. And loaded on drugs.-- In the remembrance of Herself, a New Woman and a now famous performer: "An average, tidy apartment. Only two things remained of her old life. Ornamental; a picture of two persons framed inside a valentine wrought heart. One male, short hair, a plain dark suit & tie, an adolescent. The two crooked teeth in front, the unnaturally thin eyebrows. The same receding chin. The other, the woman, in a low-cut dress, chest bare, a round bosom, a necklace. Her shoulders bare. Hair long and black, smiling."
This lyrical novel's set in the late 1950's in which cross-dressing, and being openly transsexual or gay, was criminalized behavior: "Coming home that night, a dark, svelte figure.-- She couldn't resist the urge--in her dress, secret Fatima among the night pedestrians. Tulip bulbs lit up in silver, the street. Were cool caterers of false daylight. The suspiciously angular figure scurries past the nuns convent, around the corner; a fugitive snatching the barest enjoyment out of her lavish attire, picking up her skirts & running, anticipating home. Fall had scarcely sculpted the windows with early frost, and down the street, the shadow of the great cowbell dress 'it'; wore, bobbing under his coat, which he pinched together, looking up and down the Fall tipped streets in anticipation of the patrol cops. Listening fitfully to slow gyration of tires of any passing car for fear it be the Vice. And an arrest for 'Female Impersonation'. The silver lamps were like prison lights. Awe blinding her wide eyes. Biting her lower lip (red with lipstick) urgently, icily, and heard, (thinking it was a gunshot) her murder. Her discovery in the AM, lying, bleeding to death in High Regalia on the pavements--as she set foot on the last league home, on the very steps of her apartment! The shriek of fatal discovery as they lifted up her skirts at the morgue! Only, it was not a gunshot, but the cry of a sparrow lost in the night, screaming for direction. Afloat prematurely in the dark sky. High, and blind in the blackness above. 'And may God save this soul of mine. Rich or poor. Real, or reflection... Give us this day our daily bread.'" This man Red Jordan is the 21st centuries answer to Jean Genet!

Days & nights of hustling, drug abuse, employment in a queer brothel, a stint in beautician's school, thief, showgirl, waitress, the US Military, husband in a straight marriage, and other endeavors, through which Paul tries to survive, to ultimately become Sandy, and does so, gradually morphing throughout the pages of this book in a grand processional (all too familiar in Arobateau novels) of tricks, thefts & falsifications and prayer, up to that thin dividing line --the divine Change!

A fabulous cast of supporting characters garnishes this literary feast. Red well describes age old 'Carrying's-On' of young fags & dikes clustered together in their habitats. It's fun to see the young queers of mid--century laughing and shrieking in an allnight diner at 5am, which they have taken over from the straight's, finding fun in the most barren and inhospitable of landscapes of social repression. Yet Sandy-Paul doesn't quite fit in the homosexual scene either... Here is the reaction of the astounded True gays around her: "Look at that dizzy queen!" "Oh don't! Oh she thinks she's a real woman! A fish! I saw her one time girl, tryin' to walk into the fishes toilet. Oh yes... You won't believe what she said... "Oh I forgot I wasn't really a girl!" She says it so innocent, I really BELIEVED that poor child, that she had forgot! --Until I saw her pull it ANOTHER time, down in Maxine's!" "Does she actually walk IN?" Replied the other, a lesbian. "Inside! With the fishes and everything! And then she shrieks, and runs out! With her hand over her eyes! So watch out for her!'"

Sandy speaks: "I see my own kind about me, or, what I must be with for now. Gay people. They are closer to me then anything... But I am not really gay. I am a woman, in a male body. I want a man. A husband. I want to live a life as normally as I can make it. This gay life, its allnite spots, its shows.. it is only to make do for now. A temporary place. The warmth of something."

A lot of pre-Stonewall herstory about surgeries: "The operation seemed to be getting performed in Europe, most famous-- in Denmark." And: "Now, at 28, for the third go-round I resumed my hormone treatment. They were beginning to do something for Sandy.--5cc's twice a month. A type of estrogen.--At first they were oral. Pills. Faithfully as a woman takes her contraceptive pills every day to keep from being pregnant. You put them in your mouth under your tongue and let them dissolve. They go into the blood stream through your throat. Later, the doctor discovers that shots are more effective." Also: "As she glanced around the room, she saw the instruments, the patients exam table in the next room. The sound of the nurse sterilizing bottles. The wild, impractical thought, would he do it here! Could he do it TODAY?"

This book will make you glad you are living now, and not back then in Prehistoric Times-- but, what fun they had!

Sandy's testimony in her own words: "This is my story! Perhaps very confusing. But not a bit overdone. I'll never be out on the streets again, so help me. I vowed this everytime I came off of them, and I always went back. But one thing for certain, I knew after my operation, I wouldn't, NO! I would not sink to be, such a sorry-sorry case as a woman, a transsexual who lowers herself to whoredom & degradation after spending so much effort to become a female. To dirty her new vagina by those lewd acts. That I vowed. To make an end to my career, right then."

Sandy is a fighter! --"But don't tell me of my Assumptions! I was only four years old when I began longing for girls dresses! My fifth Christmas, when I asked for a doll to play with! And a baby carriage to put her in! I've carried my grievance with me a long time!"

The reader will thoroughly enjoy this Transsexual Fiction by the Master Author of Queer Lit!

Book Review provided by RED JORDAN PRESS, 2005.

THE BLACK BIKER:

"'Shit!' Declared the black stranger. "It bes cold out heah." Said this aloud, but to herself. And it wasn't the weather she was talking about. She had a southern drawl draped in what seamed to be an adopted East Coast accent."

THE BLACK BIKER, one of Red Jordan Arobateau's Afro-Centered works certainly is an examination of black life, chiefly centered around OILS; clubhouse for that infamous dike biker gang THE OUTLAWS in all 5 in his series of books comprising THE OUTLAW CHRONICLES.

THE BLACK BIKER, book 3 of the series, has all the expected stuff-- as usual the gang goes on Runs: "Two-hundred thousand tons of steel; was the bridge over the river. RRRRRRRMMMMMM MMMMMMM! Out of the twin cone shaped exhaust pipes. The Run began at 8 AM. A thick forest of bikes with a combination of gold, red, black, silver gas tanks; and a sea of chrome & steel sparkling at the sun. Sunlight struck the sleek chassis of the black biker's motorcycle." There are sleazy sex shows, and plenty of high female misbehavior. We see again in cameo appearances some of the prime movers in the OUTLAWS gang, Daddy George, Queen Georgenia; all the Warlords, Lou, Hawk, & Rip, plus some of the cast of familiar characters, Saundra, KT, Ebony, Gerri,-- with emphasis on two of the clubs more affluent friends, African American Ross, a Senior Postal Supervisor, and old Kelly, the owner of the building in which OILS is situated. Many late night conversations are held between the two, revealing much of the dirt of the foundation upon which the Club is built. In fact it is through the eyes of Senior Postal Supervisor Ross that this story is narrated. It is the springboard on which the mysterious BLACK BIKER entrances & exits.

Ross is off on "annual five-week paid vacation" from her lucrative position in the US Postal Service, & instead of traveling around the world, for a change has decided to spend the days puttering about in her suburban home, gardening, doing put-off projects; and evenings drives her Mercedes Benz leisurely down to the clubhouse back into the inner city to sit among the raunchy, sexy, bad ass biker women. Here, Ross is a magnet to the black members & their girlfriends; as a counselor, friend, & simply a listening ear. Over the long evenings a processional of bikers (with all their pride & prejudice) come to sit on the barstool next to Ross to pay their regards & spill out their hideous problems-- mostly about $ money and failed love lives.

Then the mysterious BLACK BIKER makes her appearance: "The Mysterious Biker sat with the rest. A stranger. When she got up, clanking chains & silver buckles, lumbering off on big biker boots, Gerri asked in a whisper, "Who is she?" "I don't know," sez somebody. "But she has just broke up with her lover. She's very depressed. 'You gotta get out of the house.' I told her. That was last week. So she shows up.-- When? --Tonight. During what? --An SM demonstration. A whupping. She's trying to get over her lover, and there they are, drawing each other's blood & being brutalized, and loving every minute of it, and she gets even more depressed. She ain't into SM. She don't know a Bottom from a Top. She's already seen too much blood, flowin' out there in these mean streets."

Later, the unnamed biker, just like all the others, confides in the older black butch: "So Ross got the story. It spilled out. The mature stud wasn't sure she wanted to know, but this was the penalty of being a good listener & having a calm personality. Purple haze, tinkle of glasses then loud shouts of the bikers, mixed together in a sea of music. "So I got schooled how to stand up 'n be a man. 'N had me some fine womans, and got me some good ****. I got de best womens. I made a lots of good money in my days, an' I ain't even that old, as yo' kin see." The biker cast a sideways glance at Ross.--- "I respects yo', Ross. I don't want yo' to think of me as a criminal, or somebody low-down. I wanna make somethin' out of my life. I jes' made mistakes. Anybody livin' my life, walkin' in my shoes could have. Anybody now, anybody den. God knows. Anybody gets in a bad sit'ation, dey does thangs dey shamed to talk about. 'Cause dere ain't no MONEY." The biker looked dark and leathery; she hunched over the bar, big shoulders stretching her jacket taut."

During these long evenings we find out some pertinent facts about the Postal Supervisors life as well: "The older bulldagger looked like an undersized man. "Of course I dress for work", sez Ross. "I look hard, but I wear women's pantsuits; not much difference." She said it emphatically, fixing Saundra in her gaze. "I'm not going to feel guilty about it. Women's shoes with no heels-- they practically look like men's, but they're women's." That's what it took to get ahead in life sometimes-- compromise. A super-hard masculine-appearing dike would never never have advanced to the position Ross had. "Anything it takes to turn the trick, as the saying goes. I see lots of gay women down at the Post Office. They wear hats, wigs, high heels, skirts--bulldaggers. I know 'em, yep. Been knowing them for years. There's others could have advanced themselves in job rank but never got past distribution clerk-- that's the lowest station--because of the way they insist on dressing. --Like men. I'm butch, but it wasn't worth it to me to throw away my future."

Contrast of the po' ass broke bikers hustling up room rent to Ross's affluence & also Kelly's; the old white clubhouse proprietor (who actually owns the building OILS is in, and maintains a flat over it just to crash in those few hungover nights she can't navigate the drive back to her palatial home in the suburbs) --makes for colorful reading.

These are some of the dynamics this fine book is about-- comparisons of class; race conscious, money issues, women power, and dike validation.

You will see these issues and many, many more, examined in THE BLACK BIKER; a magnificent short novel by Master Author Red Jordan Arobateau-- a person of African American Heritage.

Book Review provided by RED JORDAN PRESS, 2005.

A BLAX MAN IS NOT A WINDUP DOLL:
Old collection. A young man's love for his golden saxophone. The dream gets
shipwrecked doing ime in jail. Facing life as an ex-con, he gets his golden horn
back and finds a unique place to play it. Was written June 1979 nearing the
end of a constant stream of non-stop creation of the late '70's. A product of re-
discovery of my black roots after spending years in the mostly white lesbian
ghetto. It involved blaxploition film-going at downtown Oakland theatre
matinees; the genre such as Pam Grier starred in, and others now forgotten.
Black music; Chaka Kahn, Bootsie, and all the black pop hits we danced to in
the disco/viewed on TV's Soultrain. I'd begun to run exclusively with an
African-American dike crowd.
I remember working on these books 30 years ago; they were written in the
office of my 3-bedroom house in Berkeley. The first bedroom was a spare,
which I attempted to rent out unsuccessfully, finally only to a girlfriend (the
blond-haired African American Marylyn portrayed in STORIES FROM THE
DANCE OF LIFE). A third room had been built onto the back of this house as
an addition before I bought it, along with enlarging the laundry room thru
which access to that room was gained. I designated it to be my office. Knocked
out a hole in the wall between my bedroom and the office making a 'suite'.
(Complete with an iron wood burning stove purchased but never installed.)
That 3rd room had poor climate control; colder in winter, hotter in summer
then the house proper. Right outside its windows was a huge Evergreen tree,
which might have caused severe damage to the property as it continued to
grow in diameter. Didn't have to worry about that however, because lack of
money forced me & my animals to move exactly a year later. In that 3rd room I
put a large table, and a desk upon which I wrote everything. The table I'd
constructed previously from plywood & 4 by 4 legs had once been the official
desk made for a different house we'd just moved out of; it had upon it about 5
wire baskets & a few cardboard catfood treys in which papers accumulated.
—Notes gathered during the weeks/months, typed up, then sorted into these
various baskets according to topic. I'd go out daily to run errands, have lunch,
do research, in Berkeley, or San Francisco, then out again at night to hunt thru
the gay clubs for a lover! Everywhere took a sheaf of paper and pen in one
pocket; notes jotted down anytime an idea occurred; or a bit of interesting
conversation was overheard, or some observation made. Beginning the next
day's work, first typed up all that material on several sheets of paper, then, cut
the different notes apart from each other, stapled each onto a separate sheet of
paper and sorted those into whatever basket/topic they seemed to fit. (A
method no longer in use, as the cutting & stapling fragments to sheets of paper
became more time consuming then merely using a fresh sheet for each
thought.) As the notes piled up, each collection developed its own book title.
As one basket grew with delicious fresh ideas, thickened with character
descriptions, came alive with dialogue, the work crying out to order itself into
chronology, my mind began to race along its topic, building a plot more
intricately, describing characters in depth, adding suddenly inspired inventions
until I began to fall in love with the work which was pulling itself together and
soon one wire basket would emerge with primacy over the others—it would be
the next novel to be picked up, transferred over to the writing desk, set down

beside the typewriter. This collection would be gone thru over & over for several days, sorted into the final chronological time sequence, last minute additions penciled in; then began to type directly from it into a novel, progressing until it was finished. During this period any spare time would be utilized to design the book's cover. When the last sentence was down on paper there was a final master copy, which was almost complete. This manuscript-master would be edited once, corrected by using whiteout, then the book was done!
I'd read it from beginning to end taking usually only a few hours, delirious for a moment with accomplishment! The next day saw me at the printers Xeroxing the master up on the self-serve photocopy machines just recently become available in shops all over the city and make 5, 10, or more duplicates of the novel. De rigueur 2 copies were mailed off to the Library of Congress, Register of Copyrights, Washington DC. Then distributed to a friend or two, hardly ever selling any.

BOY CENTER:
Old collection. BOY CENTER and WHITE GIRL! —Two forgotten books. At the time (1979) tho I had typed up the notes into a novel and printed BOY CENTER I thought it wasn't pulled together enough, but was ready to move on. This was partially because of its over-long size. So this novel remains in the stage I 'finished' or left it in, today. Originally published in 3 volumes with their pale blue covers, separately stapled together, BOY CENTER came at the end of practically a decade of non-stop writing. I'd exhausted myself. That's another reason for not stopping to rework it. Finally, changes were in the wind in my living situation. PS. Recall the day, it must have been in the mid-70's, when me, a dike, roughly dressed in blue-jeans, shit kicken' steel toed boots and probably a denim shirt strode into the paper supply company under the overpass near 14th and Mission to purchase a 'heavy duty' stapler capable of accommodating up to half inch of papers--thus the business of publishing my thick novels began. Well, BOY CENTER came about because of wanting to do, for a change, a gay men's theme work, so a lot of information went into it both fiction drawn out of years of stockpiling, having grown up gay in a mostly lesbian-homosexual world, seeing my gay brothers dance, prance, flirt, talk, and be outrageous for decades; and simultaneously taken from real life while observing the early days of a 'gay facility' on Telegraph avenue, Berkeley, precursor of the institution which is now there. Today reading back over the newly reproduced pages, I recognize some of the events as actually having happened to two dozen different people here & there scattered along life's path, tho I reconstructed & altered that material, giving them all to a few invented individuals. Reading fragments of this book prodded memories I would not ordinarily have had about those old times—the politics of them, the social climate of the rest of the country in regards to our small island band of gays; another reason which makes me glad I'm 'saving it'. As is all of my fiction work, the names/descriptions have been changed, the characters so altered so that just about anybody could recognize themselves in them, but it is nobody but the authors imagination! Its funny how occasionally people will come up to me after reading one of these books and ask; "I bet this is about

me!" because it seems so much like them, or it was something which had actually happened to them! It's a small world. Queer Galaxy is even tinier! PPS Fans may notice the similarity between this novel in which a center for gay men was established, and my book DAUGHTERS OF COURAGE which was written 19 years later which documents the rise-fall of a Dike Women's Liberation Center, with all that drama which, ensued, just like the Boys place did.

THE BLOOD OF CHRIST AGAINST THE LIES OF BABYLON!:

Old collection. There it is almost done, liberated from obscurity, all 22 volumes of ancient & forgotten lore of my salvage comprising the Juvenilia Series. I quote Robert Star from the introduction to a collection of Paul Bowels: 'Bowles greatest stories are contained in this volume, which represents the work of 40 years. There is juvenilia—some of it patently novice work along with experimentation that occasional misfired…' My own Juvenilia collection spans just half a decade. 30 works churned out…now the world has got practically all of them…. A reminder that these books complete with their little sermons might seem ridiculous, foolish, impractical, and unreal to many. Well meant, a fantasy. Idealistic above all!

 The inside verso sketch is actually the work of the real 'Marylyn' about whom much of this story is written. For her defense the title's ancient prayer is given! This beautiful blond mix-race character also appears in other shorter pieces. The 33 year old binding of BABYLON is become a stack of ragged pages plus a pile of twisted rusted metal staples which had to be removed to photocopy for my restoration program, as most of the original paste-up master copies are gone--- Pulled them out with pliers one by one. –Out of each of these 22 works composing the series (plus the other ten or 15 which had already been restored some years back—See the Lulu Series, and Alexander D'Oro & Suzie Q).

BABYLON, the novel, begins with its opening lines in Chapter One, on page 135. This means it was originally going to be a shorter story inside a single binding with several others, in one of my volumes of STORIES FROM THE DANCE OF LIFE, but like so many, underestimated, it grew longer. It opens with a line from one of my own poems, a favorite, CITY WHERE THERE'S FIRE.

It's said you have to print 1,000 copies of a book for just one to survive down thru time. From what I've seen this is true. Hence the Re Photocopy Process; because I think about all that work which went into each book I didn't want to them to get lost. The weeks dedicated to laboring over a typewriter (at least 2 weeks, more like a month, per novel). The notes and research gathered long before that. Loving the dialogue. Seeing the butch characters in my minds eye in their fancy hats, (men's), tipped ace-duce with a feather stuck in the band; and colorful suits, or their high femmes in high heels & dresses. Even in the bad ill-put together novels such as BABYLON and BOOGIE NIGHTS there is some value, for they present a too rare glimpse of dike life among the 3rd world underclass circa mid 1970's, in bars and houseparties; a demimonde unheralded.

Another constant with these 2 particular books, in both the lesbian protagonists have children. Shades of the long suffering Marionette and her sad child from VENGEANCE! A black street dike novel written around the same time, (Lulu Collection.) I want to remind people 2 things about both these 2 'Ancient' novels, which contain two special subjects; that God has extended to humans the green branch of life. And the very foundation of life is motherhood. Also that the ghetto is a place of confinement and the people locked inside it are not happy.

Have just got busted at my most recent 'free' photocopying locale; have been reduced drastically to 15 copies per day, 40 on Friday. Luckily my Juvenilia Series program is winding down with 18 done so far. These are of the last— ELECTRO SHOCK, BOOGIE NIGHTS, BABYLON, PRIMADONNA—and they are all double length books! In a quote from his introduction to a Paul Bowels collection Robert Star states: Bowles greatest stories are contained in this volume, which represents the work of 40 years. There is juvenilia—some of it patently novice work along with experimentation that occasional misfired... Hence the Juvenilia Collection spanning half a decade. 30 works churned out ... The good, the great & the bad! Now the world has got practically all of them.... Have to finish photocopying 15 pages at a time.... At that rate it'll take another 6 months....

BOOGIE NIGHTS/PARTY LIGHTS:
Old collection. Like BABYLON was partially written during 2 weeks of codeine use, which had started off for reasons of pain. (Dentistry? Or was it a severe flu?) But continued on an extra week for self indulgence, something I rarely did after my substance abuse recovery, years before. A younger Red imagined s/he was riding high and writing great during that episode, but later readings convinced him-her the story wasn't to the depths as others more well worked, nor as inspired. This is one reason it is relegated to being near the last of my Juvinille Series reprinted. Not surprisingly, its theme is one of drug addiction.

BOOGIE NIGHT'S original flaming fuchsia cover bares two photos of the artist on each of its parts respectively, by Huston photog Suzanne de Young Paul which were unaccredited at the time.

'There's no doubt we are here to party' is a line lifted from a pop song from those nightclub/disco party daze, quoted in this 1978 edition reprint. It musically illustrates the black lesbian street nightclub/houseparty scene in which these characters were involved. A milieu in which I was active for approximately 7 years. Like many of my works BOOGIE NIGHTS presents a mixed-race couple, black/Latina, similar to my own upbringing. This is one of several features I get the most comment about from fans. Sex unsurprisingly being another. Often he passes by a former site of one of his original dwellings on Eddy Street off Van Ness, then a condemned building slated to be torn down. Younger Red inhabited it upon his early years just arrived to The City, 1969, where Suzie snapped many photos. (And also down the street in the park with their dogs, where the artist had been leaping out of a tree or something...) And think of his-her early decision at the crossroad of life, wither to pursue art; writing & painting, upstairs in those gutted-out rooms, or to cross over some invisible divide, going instead up a more secure well-paved path of Civil Servant at the Post Office where he was briefly interred (to the severe stoppage of all art) and its affects on my lack of fortunes today—but, a wealth of art! Stand there and gaze at the old vision, once a lovely ancient Victorian, now a modern plastic apartment or condo building---- think of the time of choices, and of risk, of expending energy towards some uncertain future! Well, this series-reprinting machine is winding down, and once again finds the artist at his hour of decision—to settle back down into painting once again along with continuing to write? To pick up brush, tubes of oil, red, yellow, green, blue? Holding a blank canvass, ready, the easel is waiting!

C.

CARNIVALLA:

A play. Is Red Jordan Arobateau s Opus Magnus! A beautiful young transsexual woman and her best pal Red, a young butch dike flee the stifling, murderous town of Mismo by running away with a carnival SANDS TRAVELING CIRCUS--passing thru town on it s tour across the American Continent. They meet Klara Von Darling the Beautiful trapeze artist with whom a love triangle ensues; Boris the strong man, Lobos the wild man, two clowns Rembrandt & Hugo, Big Boss Sands Owner of the Circus, & his wife Judy Sands. This Majestic story is full of love, pain, fight scenes, poetic angst. The metamorphosis of Miss Carnavella is a magnificent portrayal of humor, pathos, tragedy, and beauty. This 3-act play by Master Playwright Red Jordan Arobateau is a perfect read thru for private entertainment---or see their adventures come alive onstage in your local theatre group. It makes an unforgettable motion picture. See the dilemmas, fun, and adventures shared by the queer duo in this Epic Work! Book Report provided by RED JORDAN PRESS, 2006.

CAN'T GO ON ANOTHER DAY:

Old collection. Another work retrieved from oblivion as part of my Re-Photocopy Series; CAN'T GO ON ANOTHER DAY was a discard in the left-behind-book pool, written fast, like the others, from notes; circa 1979, in Berkeley CA, taking about a month to complete. From 1975 until 1980 was a very fruitful period, living on a small bank account/insurance willed to me by my father. I reprinted older manuscripts (Where the Word Is No, How's Mars?) created new stuff, (Stories From the Dance of Life, Barrio Blues) along with about 20 other works. CAN'T GO ON ANOTHER DAY wasn't one of the fabulous books and was never reissued later. It just sat there. The print run was at the most 10 copies. 1 or 2 had been distributed hot off the Xerox press. 2 went to the Library Of Congress Registrar of Copyrights. The Bancroft Library at UC Berkeley has it. Leaving me with 2 dusty copies in an olive green file cabinet. I remember wanting to write a book on the subject of depression—with an eventual triumph thru much struggle. My collectors will want to buy this to add to their modern stuff, it's a blast from the past.

THE CLUBFOOT BALLERINA:

Old collection. Comes first in a duo partnered with THE PRIMADONNA.
Created back to back, July/August 1977; they are combined into one volume
for this edition. Both bore covers illustrated by the younger artist-author Red,
in his style of sketching done over & over throughout his crazy tormented
youth in which he learned the crafts. Back at the time of first publication they
were taken from a found sketchbook no longer available.

A reminder to readers that these books are embarrassing, (epitomized in
ELECTRO SHOCK DOKTOR for instance; the vision of hero Dr. John White
lovingly making his rounds on grim mental institutions wards might seem
ridiculous, foolish, impractical and unreal to many; -- it illustrates my
Juvenilia Series; well meant, a fantasy. Idealistic above all.) Now I find these
ramblings are so humiliating! They make me red-faced! I must be a fool to reprint them! But every now and then whenever catching a glimpse of the old
stuff lit up by blasts of light as it flies by over the face of the photocopy
machine I really enjoy it & think maybe a few other people will too. I would
edit out the profuse sermonizing stuff today, and much of the sentimental crap
I'd never print. —I'll never do this again! -- So much more reason to keep it
alive!

The end of the first book, CLUBFOOT, bares the following 'editors note':
In October of 1974, Flip Jordan began Training Sessions at RIP. The following
book, THE PRIMADONNA is the notes from her sketchbook
from Training & from Action Rap.

CLUBFOOT/PRIMADONNA is not exactly a work of fiction, but not a novel
either, as the character Flip Jordan is a semi autobiographic construct baring
an uncanny resemblance to the author (her)self; engaged in a fiction rendering
loosely resembling a group active in the 1970's which engaged in techniques of
Radical Therapy they pioneered. Flip speaks in the first person here— "I
statements"--- which is rare for Red's style at that time-frame. So,
CLUBFOOT/ PRIMADONNA stars Red's doppelganger Flip—from the
street-dike novels BARS ACROSS HEAVEN, and HO STROLL. We see in
greater detail that place where Flip, hero of BARS had gone to get help, ---that
support group of Radical Psychiatry.

 In 1973, 'Support Group' was an unfamiliar term. (The phrase used at the
RIP Collective like those of the Women's Liberation movement was 'Small
Group' or 'Rap Group'.) The idea of troubled people working together to help
themselves under the guidance of a leader with some training who might be
anybody from a trained professional down to a lay client themselves versed in
technique was a radical departure from the old template of doctor-patient
relations and all the uneven balance of power which goes along with this.

CHINA GIRL:
In the story of Charity Bing a Transsexual Chinese woman living in San
Francisco's Chinatown in the 1940's- through 2005, Master Author Red
Jordan Arobateau introduces us to one of the most fascinating characters in
modern American literature. The book is unique among the files of TG life
stories. Humorous, interesting, plenty of Gender Variant sex; & it contains a
mystery which will hold the reader spellbound. The book is the writers first
'mystery novel' though only partially so.-- The book primarily is a fascinating

32

study of a girl/boy back in these times: "And I, Charity, had brought disgrace on the family name twice! Once for acting out the role set for me in life by our Divine Creator--that of Transvesti--but second, rebelling even from that role! By my bizarre presentation of a Liberated Woman! A True Gender Variant! One who shaved their heads bald as a US Marine in boot camp, with combat Boots, yet wore a pink femmy skirt and frilly blouse--and this only signifying the turmoil inside my breast, I who lusted for a burly truckdriving man to ram me up the highway of Nirvana, yet in my very essence of heart and soul knew I would only find peace with my beloved Lotus, or some woman, yes, a bio woman, just like her! Like Suzuki. Like Emerald herself! What a divine deviant!" It portrays the conflict between Charity and her younger brother. And the relationship between Charity and her mom--Emerald. CHINA GIRL ultimately tells the tale of the love of her life, Lotus. The book is entirely set in St. Francis City by the Bay and it's epicenter is in Chinatown. Charity Bing is a good girl --she spends much of her life in the Chinatown public library.-- With these few exceptions... There are shocking references to the atrocities committed in Nanking in the Japanese war against the Chinese in the 1930's from a client Charity meets when she briefly works as a girl of pleasure in a she-male brothel in San Francisco's Tenderloin. Just as she briefly worked in Alice Hung's brothel, so she has a quick fling in 'The Red Mouse' collective, a Communist/Socialist work cell which she falls in with at the UC Berkeley campus where the industrious 'transvesti' (as she mistakenly calls herself back in that day) audits classes for free.

Most of the action of this novel is set in 1970's Chinatown. By the year 2005 Charity has survived loneliness, poverty & a broken heart & the reader gets to examine her life once again at age 60. We see Charity in 2005, ensconced in a safe small studio apartment where she is sequentially taken to tea by one or the other of her 7 friends.

The novel's highly spiritual. With a sexual edge & good humor. They live in the shadow of that ever-present threat, the 'Big One' as SF locals calls it;-- an earthquake shaking them;--a potential disaster:

"Where's your Earthquake Preparedness Kit? I want to inspect it!"

"I've just begun it dear, I don't have everything yet..."

"Do you have a flashlight? There's a rolling power outages throughout the state!"

Charity finds the box, and Delilah opens it, begins to rummage through. "Bottles of pills, good Ointment, Band-Aids--and a dildo?"

Delilah gazes up, holds the purple cucumber shaped sex toy delicately between two flashy manicured fingers. "An Emergency dildo?"

Throws it aside and digs further into the box.

"What's this?" She points to a brown plastic box nestled beneath Emergency green socks, bras, and nylon pantyhose. Ruefully unwraps it.--Inside are two bottles of female hormone pills. A bottle of liquid Estrogen Compounded Solution, and 5 syringes with inter-muscular size needles.

"Oh... Emergency Estrogen."

"Well Girl! You might want to put on some EMERGENCY LIPSTICK TOO! When the Big One starts rumbling!"

"It's in the peach colored pouch." Charity says, chagrined.

Typewritten in the original authors original font and not spell checked-this is an original first edition. This is Charity Bing's story in her own words.

COME WITH ME LUCY:
For those who don't know, is the third book in the LUCY & MICKEY Trilogy--and the conclusion of that masterwork which opens in volume 1, the pre-Stonewall, underground, LUCY & MICKEY; set in Chicago, Illinois, in 1959. In this vol. 3, COME WITH ME LUCY we discover what happens to the great cast of characters we first met in that classic dike street novel --with a few surprise additions.
The opening line: "It's been a hard life ever since I can remember. Lesbian life,--and it's never gonna quit." Is part of the private reflections of Mickey, a handsome Italian butch. "The black haired butch moved through her apartment. Mickey was age 42. The year, 1983. 25 years, and her male sex drive still hadn't gone away." The reader observes her thoughts & memories which are a testimony to a hard life. Both trials and joys.
Next scene finds that the debonair Mickey is now married to Marsha.-- "They had come in from a never-never land so fine; her and the blond in the evening dress; pretty; had been to an exclusive restaurant where they were treated well by the waiters & had the best seat in the house..." Further: "Her lady dominated the closet with dresses, a few gowns, pantsuits, and high heels." Is the part about a never-never land real? "Mickey is sprawled out on the sofa in her black tuxedo pants & jacket." And: "Marsha, round curves poured into a silk gown, on which a strap fell over one shoulder." Marsha shakes her lover awake to the reality of their lives. Their cluttered apartment. Where upon the butch: "Glances around her to get her barring, saw the beaten up sofa where she'd collapsed for just a moment, then fallen asleep. Crayon marked walls. The tiny 3 rooms their family shared." We see the lives of Marsha & Mickey & their children. Apartment they rent-- though they would like own a house. Find out about their jobs, & the savings in their growing bank account and their dreams for a lifetime.
Next scenes begin to reveal Mickey's angst--sex red hot lust driven to the point of destructiveness which is threatening to undermine the stability of their happy home. Scene after scene of Mickey after work roaming the red light district where she use to live as a bachelor, and lesbian venues --without her

beloved wife. Including picking up women at a sex club. Some very erotic descriptions in the true Red Jordan style: "The little stage is empty. Amber lights beam down onto scattered one & five dollar bills. The dancer is tired and doesn't want to work any more. Puts her short leather miniskirt back on & does up her bra and lace lingerie." This novel is at least 5 times more graphic then we dare tell in this book review! Mickey's thinking suddenly delves into ideas and fantasies which reveal a crisis of her sexual identity. Is this new behavior middle-aged angst? --Change of life crisis?

Another new event: "Then the news had come from New York. Mary Alice Leonardi had died at the age of 76 from a stroke. The estate was in the hands of the family lawyer. The family home was valued at $220,000. Car worth $5,000 bluebook price; and the accumulated furnishing of generations, antiques passed down from her great great grandmother valued at another $18,000.-- All to be sold and the money split 4 ways between Mickey and her 3 brothers. Mickey's share would be approximately $60,000."

As in book 1 there are plenty of sex scenes & memories of star filled gay nights.-- Memories of her first one true love, 25 years past-- Lucy Matusumi. Flash backs with still another of Mickey's lovers, African-American Linda, "Linda was a bisexual prostitute who worked the sex industry in the Tenderloin of downtown San Francisco a few blocks from where Mickey had lived. They had met in the street. The butch & her were together a few months while Mickey got her start in the new city." Socialists will delight in glimpses of working class routines of both Mickey and Lucy respectively at their menial survival jobs, and the political analysis Red Jordan makes. Meanwhile Mickey's aberrant dangerous sex-driven behavior has so hurt Marsha she's distraught. "WHAT DIFFERENCE DOES IT MAKE TO YOU IF I AM READING THE LOVE LORN ADVICE COLUMN INSTEAD OF SEWING YOUR PANTS MICKEY? I'M THINKING ABOUT LEAVING YOU! I LEFT YOU 2 OTHER TIMES, REMEMBER!" The upside to this dilemma; is an aside, a few pages later when Master Author Red Jordan Arobateau notes: "There is a condition called Lesbian Bed Death among gay women.-- Two women get together, they get warm & comfortable with each other, --and 2 years later the sex stops. They live as a couple, cuddling in the same bed; in a partnership, --and have no sex. This idea was foreign to the hot blooded butch. Every night sex drive pounded in her loins. --Her want. Desire came of its natural accord." In fact, this book is at least 10 times more graphic then we dare reveal!

Then the plot begins to roll: "They were preparing to go East. The flight would take them through Chicago; & planned to stay over 5 days in that Windy City which Mickey, at age 18, had first passed thru on her way to California. Where she had tarried nearly a year with a redhead woman named Lucy --4 years her senior, who she'd met at a trick show, performing a live sex act for money, & who became her love & wife & whom she subsequently left. This reminiscence began to wear on Mickey so that she wanted to see Lucy very very much.-- That out of all the girls in all the sexclubs in all the towns across the Cities of The Plain- specifically San Francisco, she'd dwell upon Lucy.--This Lucy."

The story continues with some flashbacks from the premiere novel LUCY & MICKEY. Plus odd developments to the stated reason for their trip.

"Mickey came to Chicago with a 28 year old wife in her bed. Traveling East as the seasons moved from Indian Summer into Fall. To see the sights in that town where she'd lived before. Spending half the money they'd taken over 12 years to save,--because of receiving the inheritance. Soon they would be proud home owners. Stood at the window of the hotel room, Legs spread. Trousers, jacket; handsome, hair slicked back."

We won't reveal more of this plot, or the fabulous ending to the LUCY & MICKEY trilogy. But that Mickey in her stop over in Chi--town (the Windy City) encounters some familiar faces. For instance, going down to Skid Row, one of her old haunts of yesteryear: "As she looked around the tavern, past rows of stools, broken down tables & benches along the wall, the raised platform for the band to play later in the evening; bleary eyes turned to stare at her a moment, then went back to drink. Butch dykes not a common sight here. Lucy. One of a series of half-breeds she got to know. "Lisa, Lucy and Duke. Duke Washington who we later discovered was one-quarter black. Which accounted for his perpetually tanned skin, and how he could dance."

Came out of the mouth of the tavern into the sun; hears a voice call; turns around, there's a scraggly man, skinny, disheveled clothes, a fire-water etched face, alcohol wind blew from his mouth as he yells: "BOBBY! HEY! SAY! FRANKIE! SAY!" Looking in her direction; a mad scarecrow, but with a look of recognition; while addressing her by some other dykes names. "FREDDY!" With shaky steps the man-scarecrow had jolted across the barroom floor and they grabbed each other in a hug. It had been 25 years. Held each other a moment. Freddy was a head taller, but he felt light as a feather against her sturdy body. Stink from his clothes; wrinkled, grizzly face. "GODDAMN YOU OLD SON OF A GUN! FREDDY" Alcohol had eaten him up from the inside out. No longer a sane person. The smoke & fire from hell snaked through his blue bleary eyes. Freddy staggered at her side. 'I'M MICKEY!" She yells. The name rang a bell as had her face. "MICKEY! MICKEY & LUCY! GREAT GOOGA MOOGA! THOUGHT I WAS SEEING A FUCKEN' GHOST! GREAT GOOGA MOOGA! I GOT THE JITTERS & THE HAUNTS! THOUGHT I WAS GOING ALL THE WAY CRAZY BUT IT'S LUCY & MICKEY! LUCY & MICKEY!"

The writer copyrighted this in 1991, in a feverish continuation of LUCY & MICKEY written only a few months before-- but both constructed on memories of a 'Q-Novel'--- FOR WANT OF THE HORSE THE RIDER WAS LOST, which is book 2 in the trilogy. That volume was written closer to the actual point in time of these events, around 1962.

COME WITH ME LUCY is excerpted in 2 anthologies OFF THE RAG, edited by Lee Lynch. And, A MOVEMENT OF EROS, edited by Heather Findlay. Book Review provided by RED JORDAN PRESS 2005.

COMPASSION:
Begun in Fall of 2007. An on-going journal of RJA., roughly speaking this is the 6th in his JOURNEY series of perpetual journal/diarys interspersed with small plays, and short stories inside them. Spiritual themes.

D.

DAUGHTERS OF COURAGE:
This is a brilliant novel about faith, spirituality, and revolutionary feminism. It is a beginners introduction the Radical Matriarchy, composed with high intelligence and portrayed through the vehicle of common ordinary characters. It is a manifesto wrapped in the covers of a novel. Master Author Red Jordan Arobateau has scored a winner with his DAUGHTERS OF COURAGE!
The opening scene introduces us to Valiant, a born-again Christian dike, preacher and husband, determined to make a difference in the lives of women everywhere. She is in her narrow study pondering over a Holy Bible, which she is busily correcting with blue ink pen. Later at night will continue to work on her manifesto; a plan for Women to Take Over The Earth.   First we have a little herstory of the roots of THE DAUGHTERS, which: "Had begun as an informal gathering of lesbian women-- who called themselves the Holy Order Of Mary-- in an attempt to feminize, in a new slant, the patriarchal tradition of the Christian religion which had dominated 2,000 years and to which they had little allegiance."
Valiant's relationship to her long-suffering wife Serena is well documented: "Valiant had met Serena when she was older and not a baby butch & had already wore herself out chasing after those gals. So was quite ready to be settled and a loyal husband.-- Serena. Her face was wide and full, framed by dark curly hair.-- Of Mediterranean decent. Her eyes were wide with a greenish hue. Fair white skin. A peasant body. --Serena was poor like Valiant. They were landless & of the vagabond class. They had been married for 7 years so they had a body language going between them." The butch/femme dance between the couple is well portrayed. The area in which they dwell, an underclass, interracial neighborhood across the water from San Francisco is very well described. The couple misses the companionship of other dykes, thus is motivated to form a series of groups; little church gatherings-- in their hotel room with Valiant preaching-- and finally, a radical feminist organization, The DAUGHTERS OF COURAGE.
The organization rapidly grows; they get their own meeting hall; hold events: ""We used our welfare checks to pay for it!" Some of the poorer members yelled, in a toast, clinking soda cans at the celebration. Bare floor; 2,000 square feet stretched out before them. The few folding chairs the church owned by now had been moved in. "And the bourgeoisie pays for it all!" A dyke hollered with glee." True to the Arobateau style there are many humorous passages. Also, amazingly, amid all the action there's still time for some sex scenes!
DAUGHTERS OF COURAGE begins self defense training with Martial Arts and weapons: "As they practiced pulling their guns out of hidden holsters--- imagined the safety they'd feel walking thru the night armed, instead of cringing in fear at every shadow they passed." The Daughters hold parades, street demonstrations & rallies. We are introduced to a number of interesting women. Sappho Witch, Kenyetta Nyrobi, et al.

More & more disfranchised women pour into DAUGHTERS OF COURAGE:
"THE WHITE WOMAN'S HEAVEN IS THE BLACK WOMAN'S HELL!"
Cried a voice from the back." Each woman has her own unique problems.
Can the little ship hold them all?
This novel takes on some very serious issues like incest, sexual abuse, poverty
and the failure of women to come together and form powerful organizations to
lobby in their own behalf. "We are at war! And the real enemy we're suppose
to be fighting is the patriarchy! Not other dykes!"
No radical women's organization is complete without a Dominextrix, and one
appears named Satin Lacy: "Looking good in my tiny skirt, vampish jet-black
hair & red pumps. I'm a fast girl. A Player, ready for action." --Who later
experiences a Divine Vision: "Satin was disconcerted.-- Now that she had taken
charge of her life, had her string of murders all planned, mapped on an evil
web of criss cross plane fights from city to city across America-- just to find she
couldn't ever become so evil as to be forsaken by God..."
Events thunder down towards conclusion with unforeseen twists & turns:
"What's this?" (Valiant) asks, looking up at the purple banner. They face
each other, two boy dykes, boot toe to boot toe. "WHAT IS IT?" Valiant says
quizzically; Devon is holding the pole of the banner at one end, another
familiar dyke on the other. Then Valiant just stared at her; held in her eyes,
locked-- and Devon just keeps staring back at her, behind the new spiffy
glasses of her new sporty look, body scrunched; a crooked little smile on her
face-- a sneer; not saying anything. "Lavender Avengers?" Valiant croaks
feebly once more: "What does that mean?"
Will you be ready for the startling ending of this great, as-of-yet undiscovered
literary gem?
Parts of this novel appear in Marci Shiner's BEST WOMEN'S EROTICA
1996.
PS. The dedication page of DAUGHTERS OF COURAGE reads: "In memory
of Valerie Solanas." Valerie Solanas; madwoman, creative artist, and would-
be assassin's last earthy address was the Bristol Hotel, not but a stones throw
from the San Francisco branch of RED JORDAN PRESS who provided this
Book Report; 2005.

DAUGHTERS OF COURAGE—The Play:
A play in 3 acts for 10-plus characters adapted from the novel.

DIRTY PICTURES:
A middleclass lesbian bartender—in a straight bar—finally meets a femme.
Butch/femme drama. Class differences. Interracial, white-Latina. Peep
shows. A weave of the day-to-day emotional fabric in the lives of lesbian
women. Most popular seller—2nd pub. by Masquerade. 3rd edition Lulu.

DOING IT FOR THE MISTRESS (Gay, Lesbian, Bisexual, Transsexual F*ck
Stories Vol. 3.):
Companion book to STREET OF DREAMS, this thick volume contains 3
stories, a novella, & an introduction entitled PLAYGROUND FOR
PERVERTS, in which the author, Master Artist Red Jordan makes this

politically radical statement: "I would like to express my desires-- that we need more erotic sharing between female and male. (FTM/MTF, lesbian, gay.) In all our various, colorful potential combinations of gender, sex, persona, inner girl/inner boy, etc. And that there is something queer men and former males can do to undo some of the hurt and abuse done to women's bodies by hetro males. To help heal the abuse. We need some sexual healing-- as the pop song goes. And further, to suggest that the sharing of love be between us all, and not confined exclusively to some bi polar mindset of gay only, or lesbian only. And report what I have witnessed, about the coming together of the erotic forces of female & male in the altered bodies of transgendered people."

The first story, title piece, DOING IT FOR THE MISTRESS, is a powerful work containing a lot of truth. Well worth the price of the collection in itself! A pre-trans construct about a hard butch dike, Tommy, who lusts after a voluptuous lesbian porn star/stripper-- who is under the control of her cruel and powerful lesbian butch dike mistress: "Dominique didn't participate that night. She was tired of her sport. Her big guns trained to other prey." And: "Later that week Tommy went back to the same peep show arcade, feverishly fed five dollar bills into the money slot of the video machine and the screen lit up. He unzipped his pants held his *****" This tale-- like the whole book is Hot! Hot! HOT! Dark emotions also stir: "Fate plays a strong hand sometimes. A bitter hand. It's an exceedingly hard life being a hard butch born on the transgenderd cusp of the gender line." The reader will discover the unexpected ending for themselves.

DADDY the second piece is FTM (Female To Male Transsexual)/butch love. Plenty man/'boy' sex-- flavored with SM: "ONE! THANK YOU DADDY! TWO! THANK YOU DADDY!" Boy's body quivers with the impact; small, slender; white flesh goosepimpled. A red circle appears on the right cheek. "Am I beating you hard enough Boy?" "A little harder please Sir, or I'll think you don't care." And: "Daddy's voice is changing. Lowering week by week.-- But he still sneezes in a high pitch--like a girls voice. "I sneezed at work the other day and almost outed myself." He confides, chagrined." The Arobateau Humor Machine is alive and well despite going to depths of the darkside; raunch, and hardcore erotica in this collection.

3rd is the novella length TRANSMAN RED'S JOURNEY which seems to be autobiographical..... although the author repeatedly insists that it isn't and that he often uses the name 'Red' in works which are part or all fantasy, and ain't him; IE: LADIES' AUXILIARY OF THE LEFT/CHAMPAGNE, FIRECRACKERS, GUNSHOTS, & THE SMOKE FROM THE DEATH FACTORY, AUTUMN CHANGES Parts 1-5.... Yet he states in his Introduction: "The trans story TRANSMAN RED'S JOURNEY encompasses all the heartwrenching feelings I need to portray due to our present living circumstances.-- Grief about our impending homelessness; about poverty (which has dogged my footsteps over the 40 year span of my adult life). This intertwined by race, class, more poverty, sex, and the current trans issues in my life-- which is blazing new frontiers!" Enough said! TRANSMAN RED'S JOURNEY is an education from a transitioning male in the underclass who views the world through untraditional eyes.

The last piece in the book titled FTM--A Short Piece; is just that, a quick presentation of miscellaneous facts, medical info, trans terminology, queer history: "Us young dudes call ourselves T's. But a lot of older, bearded, gnarly, heavy muscled guys who've been in transition for years have no doubt that they are men. Men totally and fully."

RED JORDAN PRESS plans at some future date to publish TRANSMAN RED'S JOURNEY as a separately bound novel, and combine the two collections (STREET OF DREAMS, & what remains of DOING IT FOR THE MISTRESS) into one, then this book will go out of print! So get it now-- it's an adventure!

Portions of this book have appeared in ON OUR BACKS magazine, and ON OUR BACKS BEST EROTIC FICTION edited by Diana Cage.

Book Review provided by RED JORDAN PRESS, 2005.

E.

EMPIRE!:

(Book 1.) Top reading; science fiction/futurist by Master Author of 60 novels. In EMPIRE!, first in this classic series, enter the world of 2056. The once mighty Am-Erica, world ruler has fallen, in its place is the advanced empire Utopia, a global dictatorship with security but no freedom, ruled by The Unity. Go to lulu.com and search for Red Jordan Arobateau & you will find this amazing gem of a novel. It is fast moving, fascinating. Great dialogue, plot, characters, and ideas. This novel keeps you spell bound, politically challenged, spiritual awakened. It has its share of sex and jaded sex. (Yes author Red is not afraid to write explicit scenes.)

Hero citizen Star1.vax~33 is a worker at a mandatory job in the Bureau of Statistics where he sits at word hole/telly processing citizen's questions. 'Starvax' is a mixed-race ftm transsexual—in a world where some people's gender has become morphed and transsexual gay etc., are of little notice. Where offspring are incubated in the mechanical wombs of SPOVA beside which sit the anxious parents cooing to their pre-designated child. Life under the domes of the Unity is well above many people's standard of today. Without a care. Food, housing (in one of Utopia's 500 floor skyscrapers) education and medical guaranteed. A mandatory job provided. An average citizen can expect to live 200 years. Be fed lies via telly and attend mandatory citizen rallies in Peoples Square. There is space travel and deep space exploration. Strange paradox in that citizens of Utopia are not entirely unhappy ...unless they believe in freedom. Just don't question, don't make waves or you might find yourself underground 40 floors dwelling sub among drones and Old Timers, and at worst, removed.

Life under the dome's ain't bad. Outside them others are living on the planet too, in dire straits due to radioactive pollution, inheritance from global catastrophes of World War 3, and global warming. Empire may sound like an overworked title for a first book in this groundbreaking series but it is very relevant, as in the text the Unity of Utopia is often compared to past dynasty's—the glory that was Greece; the Roman Empire, dynasties of the

Egyptian Sun Gods, and sadly today our own America empire challenged as it is.

In this fascinating world an adventure takes place. Young Starvax finds himself attending an underground, forbidden study group, which is gradually unearthing the lies of The Unity. In these reading groups handpicked citizens are introduced to members of the resistance, an underground movement-challenging Utopia. They are reading a study manual based on a curious document; a 'Journal'; controversial, banned, left over from the 1990's; for its past political views which are highly relevant to them now in 2056, here in this dictatorship of the modern time. Tho the reader might find some confusion at first because it laces together sections of 'the old prophets Journal into the drama itself, transpiring in 2056, (this 'Journal' is interspersed with chapters of the novel EMPIRE!) they will find them designated by a series of separate chapter numbers inherent to each. Readers begin to catch on to this technique, more prevalent in EMPIRE's first half. This 'Journal' stops midway thru, & by now the exciting drama/ adventure has fully taken hold of the readers attention. And pounds on down to its exciting finale.

Red has been a popular writer for 40 years; for his first science fiction book this is a golden gem in Sci-Fi/futurist writings. Entertaining to read, exciting for its fabulous characters, & great dialogue as well as its hard-core informative descriptions. EMPIRE! is not afraid to take on race and class issues. This book hits readers on so many fronts of interest that it keeps them reading until the end to see what happens next and at that point they will be glad to know its sequel Man Gone/ Starvax (Book 2.) is also available on lulu.com. Red Jordan Arobateau is a life long artist-writer with 60 plus novels; stories, plays, and poetry collections under his belt, available in different sites on line including Amazon.com, Lulu.com and his website redjordanarobateau.com.

ELECTRO-SHOCK DOKTOR:

Old collection. It's only fitting that here, in a book about an institution---ELECTRO-SHOCK DOKTOR—that I give credit to several fine queer & trans organizations where I've copied, for free, a lot of my inventory. If it were not for the largess of these bigger institutions which let me use their photocopy machines (knowingly, unknowingly or partially knowingly) this Re-Photocopy Series would still be undone, & its 22 volumes be stuck in their green file cabinet & miscellaneous boxes perhaps forever, never to see a crack of light or a readers glimpse at all. I originally dedicated this 2 part book SHOCK-DOKTOR to the mother who first gave me culture, and nearly drove me as insane as herself, Jane Wilkenson, who was forced to serve time in a public mental hospital, not a pretty place. If he had to do it all over again I think my father might not have signed the consent form for Jane's forced institutionalization, but in that case her own mother would have. Remember that my Mom wasn't cured when she got out; but was maybe worse. So little was known about mental illness 55 years ago, so much more advancement has been achieved today. I wrote this novel at the height of the anti-psychiatric movement, when ex-patients, the mentally ill, were targeting their abusers the mental health care professionals. A lot of the rhetoric is theirs. Subsequently then-governor of the State of California released all the mental prisoners except for the most violent/ dangerous, by defunding these hospitals, so they got out anyway with or without the efforts of former 'inmates' on the outside; with all their picketing, protesting, boycotts, literature, and radical drama played out under the spotlight of media coverage. What we see today is a tremendous surge in homelessness and many of these are ex-patients, or troubled souls who would have been incarcerated in mental hospitals in past times, now filling the streets of the biggest cities of America, SF especially—because of its more tolerant attitude towards them—formerly cared-for patients who are in practicality unequipped to survive on their own. Who have become impoverished street-dwellers. Either case is bad. Being abused inside. Being turned-out without any care or follow-up on the outside. Some parts of SHOCK-DOKTOR bothered me a lot as you can imagine, because of my personal history with the disease but I wrote it down anyway. Also purposefully gave 'the enemy' a privileged straight white male, Dr. John White, the role of hero, to fit into my idea of a universal balance in all things.

F.

FLASH ON THE HUSTLER:

Opening scene of this magnificent plot-thick novel-- descriptive of hippie era foggy San Francisco of the late 1960's-- introduces us to some of the most fascinating characters you will ever meet. "They were going to kill me. They were discussing it in front of me! They had it planned. I even knew who my killer was! Who was going to give me the fix-- a guy I'd been friends with just the night before!--" They brought Alexander out to the Pacific ocean. "My killer came up to me! But he wouldn't look me in the eye: "YOU!" Alexander said, in a voice flattened with disbelief. "Not you!" "She came to me! The wife of the Boss! If anybody I thought Delight would stick by me!" But no. Silhouetted on the beach, a figure, Delight. Her thin arms waved, a prophetess, denouncing him. "DOWN ON YOU! DOWN ON YOU ALEXANDER!" This is a rich & poetic tale set amid the swimming mists of San Francisco's colorful cut up Victorian mansions, hippie squats of that magical era. "Don't talk all 'dis negative shit y'all! Yo' ain't gonna do it now is you! Don't try to scare me! Yo' ain't gonna. You wolfen'! It's all a mistake brothers!" Cried Alexander, (slipping into black vernacular from his usual crisp white English & or Hollywood Fag accent) -- But under his toes the sea was beginning to run. Tide's come in. One mans stolen raincoat flapped over Alexander's knees, as the mass of male bodies collided. They came together. He raged against them. "AGGGGGGHHH!" Chapter 2 begins with flashbacks in which the plot is unwound for the reader to see. We come to an interesting North Beach tavern where Alexander meets a childhood friend Flip (From the BARS ACROSS HEAVEN, HO STROLL, and STORIES FROM THE DANCE OF LIFE.) "Flip's hands fly up in the air as she talks. She acts the yellow monkey that she is. As usual, her red hair is sticking out all over her head--she is haute culture of Miss Fonky Broadway." A bit more about this unusual tavern, which also serves as an After Hours club for the disfranchised literati and just plain hangers on. "Why are they here?

Because it's fashionable. Mother Mirth is The Place. Here, all the freaks and apprentice freaks. The REAL people, and their shadows. The Stars, and would-be stars--who glide beside them. The assorted misfits, and Suburbanites. Everybody else, with their hangups. They all come to get their heads into something."

The next scene shifts to portray Delight who is also a Star of the tale-- a black hippie, and wife of the Drug Lord, the Boss, soon to be his would-be killer. Delight is stunning in a Dashiki, she has ideas.

Of course as in many Red Jordan Arobateau books politics is interjected. The action returns to the strange little North Beach nightclub: "In the Mother Mirth near where the blackman sat, the tension was high. They were discussing politics. The dancer from Delano was there. Italian grapepicker. Her breasts curved in the moonlight, her chest rose and fell in a pink sweater. "Oh mercy god... How can I explain to you!" She bent over the table, and their eyes followed, watching her. "You see honey, I've fought all my life for the people. I helped blacks out in '62 and '63 with the Southern Civil Rights. Honey, last summer I was with the grape strikers. A man died in the back of my truck. I was driving him 30 miles to the nearest hospital-- that would take MIGRANT workers. Chicanos. They don't take THEM. The migrants, you understand. No money. Cash in advance. A cop had shot him honey, with a shotgun--for trespassing. It is all legal to murder you see... It was during the strike... I see how this is taking shape. John Kennedy no, he wasn't with the people yet, but he was getting recognized... He was getting identified with the black's 'cause.... Oh mercy God! You see honey, they just aren't going to let persons be free in this country! The power, the corporations-- the Army. John Kennedy didn't see it like that. He didn't believe in that shit. he was killed because he was getting too close to the TRUTH!" - Then they talked of the riots. Watts. Harlem. Chicago's South Side. Detroit."

The dancer from Delano continues: "This is America, honey, you see, life here, it's not free. The Russian peasants had their revolution because they were STARVING. The Chinese were selling their daughters. PEASANTS. The hungry people, you see? In America, this middle-class, this working class, we aren't starving... Those middle-class voters out there, they will send their pigs out to imprison their own children.... Why? Because they're AFRAID! They don't know what starvation is! They will make this country into a fascist state out of their fear. THAT''S how America will lose it's freedom. People are giving away their freedom into the hands of the pigs. The military pigs, the CIA secret pigs. The pigs are the Fascists tools..."

Among these: "radicals revolutionaries, artists freaks & just plain ordinary hangers-on", Alexander begins to speak in a strange accent: "I'm going to tell you a story, but before I get started, I want Nina Simone to come up here and sing my theme song. "Nobody Knows You?" That tune she made popular about 1958 when we was still kids going to house parties in the Negro ghetto? Flip! I don't' mean the actual SLUMS, dear, I mean the restricted neighborhoods. COLORED,-- you know, when we bought in and all the white folks moved out?-- "I met them. They told me they were into making some money. I was excited for them. To them it was something heavy. Gradually they let me in on it. Their idea of Money was $5,000! Imagine."

This special novel continues with numerous great scenes of eccentric Delights Palatial Dope Palace & Flips miserable artists 'garret'-- a one room in a Tenderloin hotel. With intricately woven plot this long-neglected Masterpiece thunders to it's exciting & poetic conclusion: "Using my soul of a criminal, I shoved a chair up against the door, so I could sleep without being disturbed by unwanted company. But instead of sleeping (for I was expecting burglars) I blew out the fire-exit door, swift as the black autumn leaves."

"SO you see, I'm running. Running from those maniacs now!" he hit a side street, scattering rats. A black figure, a desperate expression. He moved in the shadows. Raincoat flapping over his tall skinny frame. Purse over his shoulder made of burlap-- Alexander Girls traveling bag."

"Flip started in her seat. All that coffee had thoroughly wired her nerves. So Flip called out to him, "BOOGER!" And as Alexander turned, looking for the direction of her voice... she saw desperation flirt on his face. "I glimpsed it, peeking out of the corner of his self-assured mask. And this glimpse made me more afraid then before, for suddenly, through all the third Reich, through all the goose-stepping columns, the police, the army of WACS and WAVES; and behind me, my ordered, sane life-- as I reached back to get him a chair and met his eyes, I peeped into the keyhole of his soul, there was SEAWEED in my fingers! As he walked towards me in his Vaselined-back hair, I realized he was the dead man come back to life!"

As the dedication page of this book states: "This is a tale told by the hustler, full of peoples sound & fury. It may resemble the living & dead, but it signifies nobody."

Book Review provided by RED JORDAN PRESS 2005

FISHERPEOPLE:

Is Pulitzer Prize winning material. Reminiscent of Hemmingway's Old Man and the Sea.-- Step by step Red Jordan Arobateau takes us through the life of Senor Alverez. His daily routine with his animals, his yard, and his past as a young migrant farmworker in the Salinas Valley: "Senor Alverez had once been a big man, tall, medium weight; but now stooped, thinner. 6'3". Brown skin, thin white mustache like a line against his swarthy skin. A Chicano. Tweed pants of gray, an olive green jacket; his cowboy boots had Cuban heels, high ones, black & white bucks like saddles. Senor Alverez and Senor Poochie. See them making their way down the road. Senor Poochie. She was a refined dog, yes. Walked with an even gait." Sometimes the writer frames the conditions under which the old man dwells like a social scientist: Senor Alverez lived in very troubled times. Crime. Political upheavals. The beginning of the widening split of lower and upper classes--between which the new striving middleclass was being wrung dry like a rag. He lived in a predominately poor neighborhood, few whites, a lot of Mexicans, some blacks and Chinese. Mostly older people in the houses which they owned. While the young were in new apartments going up. Among them, the wild ones who hung around Main Street. He'd been in the neighborhood a long time." We find out the essentials of his life, his family, now grown & flown. And his daily worry -- getting food for his table: "One thing to know about Sr. Alverez was his backyard. Behind the 1 bedroom house was a broken down lot filled with

assorted junk. Fenced areas--which had once been even rows and paths,--now the grass was everywhere and blew like wild green hair with the wind. A hen coop built of spare lumber, rotten with age, wire sagging, rusted; feathers & straw caught to it like moss to branches. The hens were old like he was, seldom laid an egg. He'd been meaning to buy a handful of chicks and begin raising a new batch... 5 of them; Conchita and her bunch. Corn grew in the garden, striving for water among the weeds. Artichokes-- a perennial grew along the border. The same vegetables he had harvested in his youth in the Imperial Valley. Lettuce, beets, turnips, spinach, strawberries. Many were rotted, devoured by bugs. But the bed still produced--and were tasty even when partially green. He fed the animals vegetables from his garden; the dog & chickens that is; the snotty cats turned up their nose. And fed the cats an occasional egg the chickens cracked by mistake, scooped it up in his wrinkled brown hand out of the straw. People with land don't starve to death in California. There is food to be grown all year 'round." A mix of peripheral characters surround the old man, who are quite interesting; and, typical of this author, there's lots of great dialogue: "The way he'd gotten Nino; he was standing in his front yard & Hattie in hers, just having passed by each other and stopped to say hello and remark what a warm day it was, and about the latest crime in the neighborhood; when a baby kitten came stumbling across the lawn. Pitifully thin, on shaky legs. As if by the hand of God, the kitten meowed, and walked straight up to Theodoro. "There you go." Hattie remarked, or something to that effect. "I can't take it." The old man had said stiffly. "I already have too many cats. I have... Cinco." He held up 5 fingers. "Of course you can!" Hattie said sharply. That ain't too many! I knows folks who has 10, 15 cats!" "But I have too many!" He protested again, looking down a the pitiful kitten as skinny as a skeleton with huge liquid eyes begging for mercy, for it's life. "Oh no you don't! 5-cats, Ha. That ain't nuthin'. The lady down the street, look how many cats she got! Her yard full of cats! They suns themselves up on top her house!-- So you can count every one of 'em!"
 Senor A's poverty is documented: "His pension check was due. He had saved two potatoes--the last--from the sack, to plant. ---Cutting out the buds, or eyes, & set down into the earth of his garden to make more potatoes. But he got so hungry he sliced & fried them in grease & ate them. "What am I going to do?" Questioned Senor Alverez, pacing the floor. "What am I going to do? No money. Dog hungry. Cats hungry. I am hungry." And the simple idea flowed to him, smooth as waves in a tide. 'I will go fishing.'"
We read with interest his history as a young man in the fields: '8am. The ground crew had already been picking for an hour since daybreak. Picking fruit by the pail. Cutting lettuce at 20 cents per carton, two dozen heads in each. With knives they cut heads off their stalk, took off the broken leaves around it, and put it in a carton that traveled on the flatbed, pulled by a tractor thru the fields. Huge cauliflower's. Produce to stock the supermarkets of the cities." Soon, Love comes to the romantic Theodoro: "There in the Imperial Valley he had met a beautiful Chicana. Lupe wore Indian dresses, Colombian style jewelry, blue Topaz set in silver, and imitation red Rubies set in tiny crucifixes in her pierced ears. Braided hair. Her Indian face dark

complexioned. Lupe was very impressed by the Rose.. Her boyfriend was a dreamer."

 Descriptions of the ocean. The fishing are so palatable, this novel transports you THERE: "Cold windy day at the pier. Big white splotches-Gull droppings. Ocean made it's noise slapping against the pilings of the pier. Steady breeze from the south. Gulls landed on the rail. Majestic birds, white feathered wings outstretched. Sky was greyblue, identical to the water. Near the end, out into the ocean, he found a booth in which he sat. It smelled of stale piss. And empty cans of soda underneath; a fishhead, and rusted hooks."

FISHERPEOPLE is also a very spiritual book: "He was hungry to follow after Christ. He was hungry to go walking across the water on spirit feet into the setting sun, to see his Maker. Hungry for relief. For salvation. For the end of troubles. Fishing. For a few dollars passed over the wooden counter; racks of flys and casting reels & rods and hooks and snells, hung from the ceiling, or on shelves behind glass in he dusty little shop; put to use. -- They say the water is the home of the Spirit. We are baptized in water... Born in water. Conceived in water. They say we evolved from water... That life walked up from out of the sea millions of years ago. The old man looked into his heart and saw the thing he wanted most in life-- 'Master, I want to sit by You, by the sea of Galilee.'" Like many Arobateau's stories, there's a twist at the end. Dedicated to the author's own father, you won't forget this wonderful tale & its deep spiritual insights; another human portrait by Master Artist Red Jordan. Book Review by RED JORDAN PRESS, 2005.

FLEAMARKET MOLLY:
Old collection. FLEAMARKET MOLLY, GARBAGE CAN SALLY, ASHCAN BETTY; those names are all driving me crazy trying to keep track of which is which. Sally, Molly & Betty were not triplets—not even in fiction. This Re-Xerox Project is 22 books that never made the grade. Am nearly finished—6 more left to print-- but here sits Molly still a pile of papers lagging behind her sisters who were re-photocopied, cut, bound & sit in a box waiting to be shipped out to the 4 winds—God knows where! To whoever will have them! My continuing saga of biographies of fictitious people continues in this 'Scavenger Trilogy.' Some of these biographies are molded after several known acquaintances all combined into one, others entirely an allusion of imagination, enriched by general research. Molly is just that, total fiction. My 'research' was done while actually trying to hustle up rent monies at the fleamarket. Took my notes out at there in the cold air, amid stacks of used goods of unimaginable variety. The fleamarket can become an ongoing event. A perpetual motion machine; because in this affluent society stuff keeps coming to you. —IE, one can go to a fleamarket with just their own selfs crap; but during the selling day find discarded boxes of usable stuff, enough to return the following week with even more stuff along with your own crap which didn't sell before. Must remind people of the uneven pagination of all my books--- so the original page 71 is 77 then continues on back at 72 etc, so your copy isn't malfunctioning, it's the original master reprinting out the same tired mistakes into infinity. PS just finished reading over an old stapled

together Molly & told myself: 'its not bad, its not bad at all!' These books of the Juvenilia Series can be a lot of Satisfying Fun!

FOR WANT OF THE HORSE THE RIDER WAS LOST: For some reason this is categorized under the W's.

G.

GARBAGE CAN SALLY:

Old collection. GARBAGE CAN SALLY is the longest of the SCAVENGER TRILOGY. Proceeded by Molly, followed by Betty. Did the author (myself at age 39) really recycle aluminum cans, glass bottles, & process found junk for money on the level of such desperation as his (her) 3 heroines? GARBAGE CAN'S cover depicting a destitute woman of the 1930's Depression years snapped by Dorothea Lange (unaccredited) does not fit the contents of the book. Here is a photograph of a working class (laboring) woman in dire straits, tending to her babies as well as she is able—not the seeming 'by choice' drop-out-from society like Sally Del Rouge. It was as close to the subject matter that I was able to access quickly (in the constant insatiable need for covers for these novels, poetry chapbooks etc. which come spilling out). Well, yes I really did sink quite low late in that decade of the 1970's, living a much too isolated life, having spent the last of my inherited money while concentrating on writing & the paraphernalia which can go with it—buying topical books for research, typewriters, Xeroxing—not to mention the necessities of life-- and having renounced my short-lived lucrative criminal dope growing business, but not being gainfully employed; suddenly I ran out of money, woke up to realize my house was about to be foreclosed. This was just before starting back in the job market—the home health care field, by which I raised myself back up again into civilization. Yes, the vegetable gardens and chickens of FISHERPEOPLE were in my back/front yards in Berkeley. And spent a certain amount of each day collecting recyclables out of the streets. Am sorting thru about 60 banker boxes which have been with me since Sutter Ho Hotel daze, found some scraps of notes, about ASHCAN BETTY written on the backs of receipt stubs of a Business Checking account from when I first went 'official' with Red Jordan Press, an account on which I wrote no more then 3 checks. Since BETTY'S Re-Xerox edition is now ensconced safely in the Bancroft (it's a bound book, a wrap, a done deal) its only fitting this note be exhibited under her sister SALLY'S Foreword; as follows:

Even tho I may not like them, I try to support people trying to do good because if they try or hold back the result if they don't try---this is reflected on the faces of and children. Sad, starving in the world.

Well, back to Miss Sally. Here is a quote near the novels end; "It's a very morbid thing—that Sally Del Rouge. Because she's living a problem that's already been solved. I mean--- she is sleeping in a doorway by choice, how can you better her situation? She'll still be in that doorway!"

All I can say about that short period at the decade's end, 1979, is that this author did make the decision to snap out of the nadir of economic despair, reignite my temporarily lost religion, got an entry-level job, rejoining society and saved my soul.

THE GREAT HEART BANK ROBBERY:

The streets of New York City, 1962, Greenwich Village. We are introduced to Timmy: "a tall, good looking girl" who is cruising the gay section of the Village (before Stonewall) where the gay kids assemble from: "All over Manhattan, the boroughs. They came over from Jersey, to hang out in the streets."
Timmy is a waitress, a butch sort. A confused 18 year old. A nice kid amid the good kids & street tramps. Confused if she should go all the way gay, or try to be straight.
"Each group in this drove of gay kids, each is a messenger exchanging phrases of companionship. Each new group coming up, out of the subways, off the busses, out of taxis,-- from uptown, from downtown, from the boroughs, walking from the Hudson River side, and from the East River side-- multiplies in its great experiment. We cry back and forth to each other; birds in some haven arrived to this migratory place. Some still in flight. Some undecided. Cry like kites. "Hello! Hello There!" Passing along, cruising. Casting an eye as where to stop and settle in." But there is an undercurrent of drugs, dope; pills & fighting in jealous love triangles. Then the scene is moved along by: "MISS MARY!" Cries, squeals of gay boys with peroxide hair, at the sight of 'her' blue uniform; "ALONG COMES MARY!"
Then Ellen, fabulous Ellen, arrives by taxi, exits it theatrically. Ellen is a decent girl. She is immediately surrounded by her fans and admirers. Soon, Jackie a 'Drag Queen' comes on the scene: "Jackie is about 28. She picks up tricks in Times Square, or 5th Avenue, or Bryant Park, where the New York Public Library is, in upper Manhattan. She is a man posing as a woman. She didn't wear any make up, just the wig, and the falsies. Too frantic to stop."--As Arobateau describes it: "I'd like to tell you about the already tiered boys, street-used. Who are just hustling enough for a meal, because they're not pretty. Skinny butts, in their rumpled clothes." Occasionally a gang of dikes walks up a few blocks to hoot & howl up at the girls up inside the stern brick building the House of Detention.
Timmy crosses paths with a middle age man who hangs around the scene: "One of the main johns who came down here to buy young meat--he was a heterosexual-- was the head State Psychiatrist of a nearby state. This job he had acquired by having a doctors degree, money and connections. The man was really sick. And down on the streets cruising in his $15,000 convertible every week to catch some young girl, or maybe a boy." After receiving an impromptu 'psycho-analysis' from this pervert Timmy is even more confused about her life.
Gay kids, & gay street kids, they all play together in the streets. Timmy is cautious. Undecided. And returns home alone-- but still thinking about the lovely Ellen. In the subsequent days, while hanging out, the kids notice some odd goings on of two suspicious men who have the fortune/misfortune (depending how one views it) to be living above their hangout, Pam Pam's Restaurant, outside of which up to 100 gay kids congregate. The two seem to leave their apartment walk around looking suspicious, then return; just to

come back out, every few minutes. Are the undercover cops? They seem to be casing out the bank across the way!

Throughout subsequent days, Timmy meets up with Ellen again, in the tumultuous street scene assembled around Pam Pam's; in the gay bars and Washington Square park. She cruises beautiful femmes, tosses and turns in her young mind as to which road to travel. --As well as keeping notes on the two mysterious men, and their assumed bank hoist. She attempts to solve the mystery of these would-be bank robbers.

Timmy interacts with some interesting characters in some very emotional exchanges of teenage angst, in which older people attempt to 'figure out her gayness.' And advise her 'what she should do about it.' Although primarily interacting with her own kind--the gay street children with all their humor, hustling & great expectations. Sometimes even panhandling to supplement her waitress job: "They stood. A gang, under the eaves of huge New York buildings. Loitering. Hooting at passerby's. Timmy's feet hurt awful, from nearing the end of the week, constant walking. But it was too hot to go home and change. Sweat dripped down her back and her uniform stuck to her pink thin body. Bare arms and legs sticking out of it. She hadn't been in gay life long enough to get freaked out by other gay kids seeing her in a dress--work clothes. "Timmy! This is my lousy name ! I wish I could be somebody else for a while!" "Well be me! I need the company!" A little rough dike says, loud. 'Lousy fuckers.' (Timmy) looked desperately out at all the full grown people passing around them, imprisoned in their dresses and suits and ties. "They give me a pain up my ass!" Timmy commented, and turned, and spit shreds of tobacco from her hand-rolled cigarette out on the pavement. Another reason she wanted to stay out here, she was broke. Payday was every Friday. Today was Thursday. She'd only made $1.30 in tips today. 15 cents busfare. 10 cents for a phone call, left her barely a dollar. Hunger would hit her later that night.-- "Well I need some bread man... You got some bread Mister? Whoops!" A butch propositions a butch next to her-- in joke. "Yea man, you and me both. I'm broke as a joke." Says the other dike, hands in empty pockets, jingling her keychain, the only metal there to make a sound. "Man, I'm tellen' ya', lets pull a job." One says. "What kind of job? "Hell, I don't know. Wait 'till it's dark, grab some fucker in the hallway and beat shit out of him!"--- A good looking woman walked past, and one ugly little squared off dike took off from the pack and began following her, hands jammed down in her pockets, following this poor straight woman along the avenue. The woman wore a dress, high heels, and looked like a very cold mannequin. "Hey baby! Do you want a thrill! I CAN GIVE YOU A THRILL!" She whistled thru her teeth, 'till the annoyed woman disappeared in the crowd. The dike came back, lounging, like she didn't give a damn. ratty, but disappointed as usual." "WOW!" Says one of the girls. "That's neat!" A woman passed a few yards away, stockinged legs crossing scissor like. She was a splendidly built mannish woman, about 160 pounds, dressed in a blue light satin suit, that softly rounded over her full bosom, strong hips and thighs. Tan and brown sporty heels. Trim legs. She looked like a woman who was good at sports. Soft hair caressed her face. But there was more. Bronzed. Bullish, yet soft. Her eyes, were deep and gave off a warmth that most women walking thru this crowded street didn't have. Poignant. Like she was REAL person. A swing to her walk. This woman looked hip. There is a rich, sporty, warm air about her. She is free. Maybe she is a successful show girl. She has a strong worldly face, and short blond curly hair. "WOW!" Said another, sizing her up. "HEY MOMMA!" "Looks more like daddy." Said another. "Hell! She can get on top of me anytime!" Responded another. "HEY MOMMA! LET'S LIE DOWN!" "SAY! BE COOL!" Says Timmy, wide-eyed, "I KNOW HER!" Scenes of a hot Manhattan summer. Again, Timmy meets the fabulous femme: "The next evening, Ellen appeared early. Well made-up. A printed shift on, and her black glossy hair groomed out in a beehive."

A gay memoir at its finest! You will love reading this historical book & all the adventures in it.

Book Review provided by RED JORDAN PRESS 2005.

H.

HIGHER GROUND:

A semi-religious based 3 act play; in which the gay renters in a flat suddenly discover their landlord has rented the other side of the building to 2 anti-gay churches. Humorous & dramatic. The tenants include 2 gay men; dikes; one MTF transsexual; white, black & mixed race characters.

HOBO SEX:

This short read, written by the Master Author of Queer Literature in 1991 bares a picture of him--prior to transition-- in a photo from the '60's on the back cover. Red Jordan was close to homelessness himself on so many occasions it ain't funny, and proves the adage that Art Seldom Pays. He has dined out of garbage cans.-- Which is sometimes higher quality then food in the Church free lines! It is rumored in a fine article by Michelle Tea which appeared in the San Francisco BAY GUARDIAN (June 23-29, 2004), that all of the furnishings in his studio are 'found' objects, discards from the streets of Empire.

HOBO SEX is about just that-- dumpster diving. It is about two disenfranchised white women,--part of a 4th world estate right here inside the borders of the richest country on earth. One of them hampered by being young, the other, mentally challenged. Diana has made appearances in other of Red's writings-- notably THE HERMIT in the long ago feminist publication COMMON LIVES/LESBIAN LIVES.

Diana is a cut above the average homeless person, as the territory she chooses to roam is Berkeley, a student area; particularly Telegraph Ave which dead ends on the UC campus; site of the demised Flower Children of the 1960's, and People's Park of the Free Speech Movement 4 decades past. Their lives together, Anne and Diana is just hanging on, daily with their dogs and shopping carts full of crap. We must warn the reader there is a lot of sex in this portrayal; as well as rotten food, and stained plastic garbage sacks. Sex- with a capitol SEX! And no holds barred!-- Nor the least bit inhibited. Amazing what two dikes can do out in the streets under the cover of several shopping carts covered by tarpaulins! There is truth and humor. Like when some snotty middle class 'dykes' catch them in their facility in the women's restroom taking a bath-- its hilarious. Mostly the book is high energy and greatly entertaining. A non stop read.

How did (AKA) Diana get there? "Her name at that time had been Clara. -- A Mother Given Name. Clara Van De Clerk. So it was bleak after her father committed suicide. Mrs. Van De Clerk and Clara sunk into poverty--of a specialized variety. Lived in a big house that was paid for by the fathers insurance, in an affluent neighborhood. Mother educated, but couldn't earn a decent living. So they starved; shared a can of tomato soup for dinner and dwelled by candlelight, having the electricity cut off repeatedly for non-payment of bills. It was an antisocial upbringing. Clara's mother was too hysterical to mix with co-workers; and took very negatively to being elbow to elbow with the stupidity of the common world."

This novel is a view inside the private/public lives of the principal players Diana & Anne and compatriots like African Queen Zimballa & her gay son. Is also a portrayal of the dezines of the street and their collective essence: "And this of course was before the bulldozers lunged thru the lot & Park, vise-jaws uplifted-as the mouth of a giant sloppy eater dripping coats & backpacks out of its iron teeth--the peoples bedrolls and tents & carts and stuff scooped it up & vomited it out into garbage trucks that sped off to the city dumps, & cemented a chainlink fence around the property & kicked them out."

More descriptions from HOBO SEX: "At first, a decade ago, when she'd been living on the streets alone, Diana's survival plan was to creep away in secrecy into a park and no tell anyone. "No one knows where I'm hiding." That was the old defense. But now Diana was too prosperous to hide-- 3 dogs, 2 shopping carts laden with rugs and sacks and sacks of clothes from the Free Box.---Possessions.   Amid bags and bags of old mildewed clothes-- older acquirements; and the cans and bottles that her and Annie Pickup picked up on their way to nowhere, bony white hands reaching from ragged sleeves and padded jackets; carts bursting with junk as they walked stoically up the streets from the lot to the Park 20 blocks off."

There's class consciousness in this very special book. The wheel of fate turns in a unexpected way: "Rich (primarily) that lived on their hill suddenly found themselves homeless. 5,000 people.... 2 billion dollars in lost homes; valued in the half million to multi-million dollar range. Luxury for it's own sake. Red Cross stations were set up and food giveaway programs for the Yuppie Homeless affected the programs for the poor. The Food Give Away held every month was delayed several days. When Annie & Diana finally lined up, after waiting 2 hours they discovered instead of the usual 5 pounds of cheese and canned goods there was only stale bread and butter. Which Diana threw down in disgust & her tiny companion quickly retrieved. "THEY'RE GIVING AWAY OUR CHEESE TO THE RICH YUPPIES WHO GOT BURNT OUT BY THE FIRE! YOU KNOW THOSE RICH PEOPLE AREN'T GOING TO EAT THIS CHEESE! IT'S HIGH IN CHOLESTEROL! AND THEY HAVE TO WATCH THEIR FIGURES!" Diana howled. "THEY'LL PROBABLY THROW IT AWAY!"

There's spirituality in this book and a lot of love: "Soon winter winds would come, wet on the ground, and wash it clean. The century would change to 2000

51

AD,--it was just around the corner. Nothing else much would be different, just this cycling, the poor always with us; women having to defend themselves, the mad, the Christian, the rich, the oppressors, the darkness that envelopes us-- and us always looking towards the Light beyond, from somewhere--that never dies."
Book Review provided by RED JORDAN PRESS, 2005.

HO STROLL:
Hookers work the MacArthur-San Pablo strip in Oakland, California. A lonely gay sistuh begins dating these working women. If you enjoyed BARS ACROSS HEAVEN, you'll like this longer novel. Black street dikes in the 1970's. Feminist outlook. Sex. Introspection.

HOW'S MARS?:
The book opens with the scene of 3 hungover dikes who have hitched a ride from two nameless men just released from prison. Their car radio blasting: "TROPICAL, THE FOURTH! $.80. $4.20, AND $3.60. AT HIALEAH, THE DAILY DOUBLE...." Boomed down the dusty streets of Philadelphia, out of the four open windows of a two-bit black car; shaky-frame, as it skimmed down the ancient neighborhood of the downtown district." It's the early 1960's when gay was still the love that dare not speak its name.--But it definitely did Carry On, in the bars, parks, restaurants and streets regardless!
"The ones in the back seat, they'd been up drinken' all night. --The three girls, so they were hot, and dizzy. Their three heads line the backseat window. In the middle, jauntily, a red beehive of hair teased to nearly a foot in height. The starlet, striking in her toreador pants, high backless cocktail hour slippers. It is Lois. Who looks like Elizabeth Taylor. To her left, a platinum blond, a butch hairdo, but beautyshop done, short cropped hair, so her pink smooth chubby neck showed thru the tail, it was JoAnne, in white khakis, gymshoes, and a blue shirt. And to the other hand, is Ursula. A plainfaced girl, medium length brown hair messy. Nondescript." They arrive at the hotel and Lois, the Star, tries to work the two men into paying for their hotel room, but the two are broke and refuse. Lois responds: "FAGGOTS! GET LOST YOU BIG TWO BIT PHONIES... FAGS! NOTHING BUT FAGS!" The car drove off fast." So Ursula, who works an honest job for a living must pay for the room. Lois complains: "It's Fucken' demented! Look at the fucking demented wallpaper!"
The threesome have a discussion as they unpack their things, revealing their past. Also, that plain, simple Ursula has a mad crush on both the blond butch JoAnne & her snappy showgirl femme Lois. Distanced herself from the Blah Ursula, Lois primps in the mirror complaining to Jo something about "the night before." Subsequently it is revealed that Lois has left New York City in a hurry, because she is on the run from a Mafia loanshark.--And what he is going to do to her if she doesn't give back his money-- with BIG interest. Chapter three flashes back to NYC, Friday, where the 3 are seen going frantically between gay restaurants and infamous Mafia owned dike bars; from one to the next: "We'll find that money before the day is out today...." Promised little Ursula, and put her arm tight about Lois."

52

The first in a sequence of rapid scenes, like a macabre Fellini picture, or a portrait of Dante's inferno is when Lois gets in a altercation in Greenwich Village restaurant with a hooker friend-- to whom Lois also owes money, in which this pretty would-be movie star receives her first slap of the evening. A portraiture of street characters. Gay girls & their baby face butches: "Good. I left her. She wouldn't listen to reason. She's going berserk. OH! That Dederia! She's so Demented! Did ya see her in there! The cops'll get her!" Lois stood, a fashion model of these streets, in front of Pam Pam's. Night had fallen. Now, neon decked the streets multi-colored as a Christmas Tree. The neon winked on and off behind them..... "Why that syndicate punk is going to kill me if I don't get him his money. Ursula, I HAVE to have that money this Week! She can do without her lousy fix more then me without my face! That Wench slapped me! .... Already he's bothering me! He MADE me give him everything I had... He twisted my friggen' arm half off! That lousy four dollars! He was gonna kill me! Then, WACK! Just like that! WACK! She really slapped me! Oh it hurts! Fuck!"

The trio repairs to the next tavern, a gaygirl/sissyboy/hustling bar. in which Lois receives a slap from the barman's towel for trying to clip a male tricks wallet.

More fights follow in more locations: "And now we have Miss Ricki. A real lesbian. Ex-hustler, of the burglary variety. Face fixed with a bit of make up, wearing the very popular butch hairdo--stripped to the roots of color, and thus turned platinum blond, like Joanne's. As Ricki sauntered along the bar talking to the kids, a drink sloshing in hand, nodding and greeting folks, out of the corner of her eye she caught something familiar. Ricki turns-- there, before her eyes, Lois stands--pressing Donna into the wall with a straight arm. Surrounded by a crowd of hostile people. "GET YOUR HANDS OFF MY GIRL!" Ricki howled, leaping across the room, upsetting tables. She snatched Lois by her blouse and covered her face with slaps, screaming, "FUCKER! MOTHERFUCKER!" Lois snatched herself away... Ricki went at her again. "FIGHT! FIGHT!" Cried the women, cheering, howling and laughing. Another girl grabbed Ricki from behind. The two fell, squirming on the floor her skirt up, holding the other down, arms and legs wrapped around her like a crab."

Friday night is filed with wild antics, altercations, in which the poor starlet is slapped dozens of times, but she is fearful of a far worse fate at the hands of the syndicate stooge. Until finally as the night is endings, tho still unsuccessful to find money, they escape by Greyhound bus to Philly intending to continue the non-stop party at a gay bar there, newly opened-- when night falls Saturday. They find themselves disembarked in the stony caverns of downtown Philly, hail their 'cab' and the story continues to its exciting climax! As all of Arobateau's work, the reader will never fail to be entertained by this underground street drama worthy of it's place in gay history.

Book Review provided by RED JORDAN PRESS 2005.

HOW DON JUAN DIED:
Old collection. Is referenced briefly in my novel WESTPOINT OF THE UNIVERSE by a character, race-sensitive, who states, "I thought it was a

prejudiced little book…" If that reader had bothered to skim thru this slim play to its final page they would have found authors notes about 'correct politics' explaining the racism, sexism, anti-Semitism & fat phobia of its actors. DON JUAN is a character study. This 'disclaimer' on Red's part is followed by a great example of little 'sermons' he/she use to inject into writings of the '70's after a recent white-light dawning of religious conversion. The verso of this dramatic work bares the copyright date 1976, which makes it one of the earliest of the Juvenilia Series; and something else quite telling, the copyright claimant is listed as Red I. Arobateau (instead of the initial J.) So it was as a young artist he'd begun to envision his name cemented into history and completely changed the middle by substituting Jordan, (from his grandmothers line) for the one formerly given him by parents, probably his mother, unsuspecting of his true gender nature. Finalizing it into the aristocratic Red Jordan Arobateau. I remember the idea for this play came from article in a newspaper about 4 teenagers who had died in their stalled car on a snowy road one night. Decided to imagine what might have been their last thoughts & mistaken actions-- combined with my own personal stuff I needed to vent-- so this play in no way should resemble anybody living or dead----just the sad situation of the 4 parties involved.

A HILLBILLY CHILD IS LIKE A BUTTERFLY:
Old collection. A nine-year old tomboy struggles with her family to keep from being separated from the love of her life—the Girl Scouts. Her family, fresh from Appalachia, is threatening to pull up roots again, leave the big city and go back home. HILLBILLY CHILD is set from memory of a building me, Dog Brown, & an ex-girlfriend in a larger unit, lived in in North Oakland, (beside the Macarthur Boulevard whore strip). Recall the people in the building, mostly poor whites, many recent arrivals from the rural South. And modeled BUTTERFLY after them. There's quite a bit of class conscious in this. A low-income shabby redbrick kitchenette racially mixed, tho less blacks and more whites; not like some of the low cost residence hotels blocks further west near the Downtown sector which were all black. -- In which I feared to go myself, and wisely used the option of light skin privilege to reside in a place where by color I did not stick out like a sore thumb.
In the later part of the 1970's after writing a string of blax novels and more autobiographical stuff (HO STROLL, WESTPOINT) I wanted to reach my imagination far into a new ethnic/class group I knew little about and envisioned HILLBILLY CHILD. Was to repeat this 26 years later with my transgender hero Billy Bradford of STAGE DOOR, also with hillbilly roots. The small amount of copies-- the minimum necessary—means it was near to the end of my non-stop rolling-off-the-press book production   which screeched to a halt with the loss of the Berkeley house and a swift relocation to a low-income fringe neighbored in the city of San Pablo on the Richmond border. In that shack suffering poverty, but now newly readmitted to the minimum wage working poor, eating better on food stamps, commuting by bicycle to the end of the rapid transit station; complete with the notes for CHINA GIRL sitting in a wire basket on my table. (Remember the story of not having the energy to complete CHINA GIRL then, this point marks the

54

beginning of the 11 year span in which I wrote nothing at all Absolutely nothing.)

Now, halfway thru my Re-Xeroxing Project assembling its final novels, I locate my personal copy of HILLBILLY CHILD IS LIKE A BUTTERFLY with a lime green cover and scratch & apply lettering; find there is only this one left. Am sure just 5 of these were printed, having run low on funds. —2 went to the Library Of Congress for the copyright (something I can't even afford to do today in 2006 for the recently churned-out products of my book factory). Another was searched up out of the file cabinet within the past decade and sold to the Bancroft. Which leaves only one more, probably given to a friend R, during those years, the mid-to-late 1970's, who got a free book every time a new title was finished. R. claimed she read each of them. We'd most often meet in the gay church or I'd drive by her house in the Projects with a stapled copy of it. A week later, I'd ask again had she read my latest and what did she think of it? Every single time she said "Yes I did. Yes I read the whole thing! I like it. You know like all your work." Maybe. I'll never know if this sistah was telling the truth. Have not mentioned this fact before tho it's been sitting in the back of my mind…. I'd finish a novel and this friend R. would get that one copy. She was my only fan.

I.

INHABITANTS OF A GHETTOIZED POPULATION:
A play in 3 acts, 10-plus characters. Transexual. Colorful, hilarious, tragic; full of divas, swaggering FTM's, straight parents-without-a-clue, corruptible cops and more. High adventure on a small stage.

THE IRON WOMAN:
2nd of Red Jordan's 2-volume poetry collection., which contains all of Red's poetry—both verse, & vanguard style. THE IRON WOMAN begins in the identical format as Volume 1,. THE AGE OF OM. Lets start with the cover, a sketch by the author (also a Fine Arts Painter); next, the verso with a list of credits of small chap books Red self-printed by mimeograph, machine copy, & stencil 'back in the day' before Xerox photo copy, which he distributed in the streets and gay bars. The next page, a paste-up photo of him as a 24 year old, by photographer Suzanne De Young. As in Volume I, THE IRON WOMAN is divided into sections. These are listed on the next page, Table of Contents. First there are General Poems, some very complex, some dating from 1957 when the author was 17. (His earliest work of any kind.) Then Women's Liberation poems from the 1970's. The third section Epic Poems which run numerous pages. Then, a Blues Section; basic rhyme poems of the 'she done me wrong' genre. The end of the book is reserved for God Poetry and also Later Work including some street hustler poetry. At the end of this thick book is an index of titles in alphabetical order, listing approximately 350 poems. They include pages-long epics, to simple haiku's.
From, DEATH FAMILIAR:
> September is red; pale.
> The peeks of Autumn, burning.

The raise of materials of soil
  to asylum, in a zenith!

Across the barest boulevards
  my bran reaches
  on some empirical return
--amid the scuttling cardiacs;

As a Swan from an ugly Duckling,
        Sight arrives!

Dear Mercury spreads her wings.
      So molten!
        Breathfull!

From, THE HUMAN ANALYST:
      Now, a fishing village, or now we sail.
       New expansion, revolution.
      Now a dynasty troubled by no lords.
      Raintones, swamprain evoked some particular works.
      Survey in storm, human race in trial.
      Each of us
              Separated from ALL, by a breadth of
      Understanding.

      From each pot-shard stratus
       This force that comes thru unconscious zones-
        -breath behind my spine
        from a gene signal; Each tiny fire
        where there ashes now.

      A stone, a skill, an arrows ash.
              Their first steps, my base.
              My trend, their grandchild self.
              My last sign, their end.
              First traveler is last dead. That boatman
                ferrys on. Departing, we sack our crude
      implements
              We move again from the radius of the first camp.
              Each story, each person's look is a campsite
      welded
              in something tougher then rock.
              A dish, a skull, artform on wall;
      Rain older then fossil, drums both my earbones still.

From I SAW A SAVED SISTUH:
       I saw a woman who use to whore down
       on the whore stroll on MacArthur Boulevard

56

when I was a trick, running in & out
 of them motels with rainbow ads
 green, red and yellow M.O.T.E.L.
 arm and arm with some girl,

The first 2/3rds of the book is secular, however at the end is religious poetry.
Everything from high verse, as THE DEATH, THE CHRIST, THE LUST FOR
LIFE! To, GOD FOR CONFUSING TIMES. And, JESUS FOR THE FAST
LIFE.   Book Review provided by RED JORDAN PRESS, 2005.

IN THE MAELSTROM:
A play. Old collection. IN THE MAELSTROM should be added to the
collection of Arobateau plays. Originally called a 'Story-Drama' this 30 year
old text is part of my Re-Photo Copy Series with no attempt at editing, only
reproduction to save it from oblivion. It was written around 1962, ten years
before first publication; carried in manuscript from Chicago to San Francisco.
The play contains a few more characters then listed under Cast; as a younger
author assuming only the principal actors were supposed to be mentioned.
Prior to this time only 2 copies remained in my possession.

J.

JAILHOUSE STUD:
The blurb on the back cover of JAILHOUSE STUD reads: "Prison is a huge
factory. A fortress made of gray stone. Bars from bottom to top. Guards in
the towers, with rifles. Screens on every window. Windows spaced out evenly,
in rows. Behind each is the prayer of a woman: "I want to win! I want to be
free!"
In the opening scene JoAnne Woods stands before the judge in a courtroom in
Los Angles, California. She is 'in drag': "Jo Jo looked different then anybody
would have ever remembered seeing her--had there been any friends or
relatives in the spectator section. Big; a stocky build, black skin, the 22 year
old was wearing a skirt, blouse and sweater; ill-fitting. -- Jo Jo's thick nose was
dabbed with a tiny trace of powder-- to keep the sweat from turning her black
skin shiny like a Seal. And, she'd taken her nose ring out. Eyes painted in a
hint of lady make up. The Public Defender was at her side. "JOANNE
WOODS, YOU ARE ACCUSED OF SHOPLIFTING, HOW DO YOU
PLEAD?"
Soon we see Jo Jo disembarking a jail bus into women's prison. Now clothed
in a blue uniform dress with other inmates handcuffed in double rows. We are
introduced to Guard Knorr. "The matron led them down a cold drafty hall.--
She was strutting in her gray uniform. Her mouth twitched at the corners,
almost breaking out in a selfish grin of power.-- Females. A sea of them.
Sitting on their bunks, or, in larger dorms, at tables-- metal slabs bolted to the
cement floor. Young fast talking slicks; arthritic old horrors in their 70's. All
dressed in the same blue uniforms. Sometimes the noise was deafening. There
was no privacy. Yet, oddly, it was a lonely lonely place."

We begin to meet the other prisoners: "Rosie Sanchez was in for Murder 1. Cookie. A white woman from the near-poverty class. She had a medical condition--Diabetes--at the border-line state. Judith was in jail for demonstrating against the Vietnamese war. This Jewish woman was in for political reasons. 70 days. Desiree was a stripper, in for indecent exposure. 60 days. Tall, brown and attractive. Desiree had a regal baring and many lesbians secretly eyed her; both prisoners and guards." The plot begins to stir with new found friendships building behind prison walls.

"Jo Jo's hands were empty. She was poor and couldn't even afford a cigarette. Down the brick wall she heard the melodious voices of two fish talking. The stripper was saying; "I got my money already. $1,000. It was to advertise for the porn studio." She wiggled her curvaceous body demonstrative. "$1,000. I took my clothes off in the middle of Venice Blvd.-- They had a float in the parade. That was at 12 noon. At 2pm they bailed me out, and by 3 I was out shopping."

Interjection of some of the more detestable prison guards begins to add fuel to the plot: "Footsteps clicked primly down the hall, the shadow of the female guard Knorr. She liked it on the block with the girls. They obeyed her or went to solitary. Knorr was a nervous and high strung woman. Tiered easily of being cooped up in the guards cubical. She too was trapped behind prison bars-- 8 hours a day. ---She walked the halls like a cat pacing on a hot tin roof, looking for trouble."

The first night in lock up something bad occurs. "Minutes ticked on into hours. 1am. Many fish still had not found sleep. Suddenly, a scream rent the fabric of night. A loud scream, it was not play. Folds of sleep drew back revealing a skeletal backbone of fear as many women rubbed their eyes, awaking. It was a hideous scream that went on and on, lungs filing with panic and exhaling shrieks-- like someone being beaten or tortured. 'AAHHHHHHHHHH HGGGGGGGAHHHHHHHHHH!!!" --The scream was ice cutting. It penetrated into the psyche of the entire women's prison. "AGGGHAHHIGHAGHUIUUA HHHHHHHHHHOGGHHH!" As the guards dragged Cookie down the waxed corridors to the basement."

Differences & rivalries between the prisoners becomes apparent: "They had only been in 10 days when some shit started. Jo Jo was in the laundry room with her dorm and 2 other dorms getting clean uniforms when she saw Desiree. They smiled and Jo began to talk. Suddenly a redhead butch, black, with an evil expression butted between them, shouldering her way; "I DON'T LIKE WHAT YO' SAYIN' TO HER! MOVE IT, GET LOST!" Later Jo Jo saw Desiree and Cadilac with their heads together laughing, & the short redhead cast a dark expression at Jo Jo across the room which made her wonder; was that a set-up from the beginning? Whose side is that Stripper on?"

Later another habituate of the block is bussed back in. "Coral was 22. Very fluffy and femme. Her hair was long and streaked blond. But she was a bold sister. --Some of the white cons hated Coral. Wanda, the attractive forger sat with her group of 3 other long-term white cons. Evily they looked upon Coral who was gabbing along with the blacks in a black accent. Wanda & her gang sat at the smaller table--for they'd been displaced from the best table (in the day room) by the ever-increasing numbers of blacks. For years the best table had been theirs. Wanda blew smoke down her chiseled nostrils."

We are introduced to their problems here in the women's lock up:
"The largest group of offenders were the prostitutes. There was Eleanor Jenkins, a black sister who had acquired this street name of Kitty Twat. Over years of selling her sex in the streets she gradually came to BE Kitty Twat. After ten years of whoring and arrest, and re arrest, now she had a new title-- number #3017464.--

The second largest group are the drug traffickers: "It was the most cutthroat of the girls who were involved in the narcotics trade within the hollow cells behind the stone walls of La Habre. --- When Kitty Twat's 6 months sentence was over two men encased in metal-- a $20,000 Bonneville Cadilac car-- would glide up like death to the front gate of the prison; hat brims over their eyes, stern faces, nodding in time to music's cool sound of black jazz. Her limousine dope dealers would glide away with her as undersea fish gliding thru the night, predators with luminous eyes hunting for prey. And carry Kitty back to Los Angeles, drop her off at a curb on Hollywood Boulevard to continue her prostitution & minor drug sales."

The story begins to mix it up. The drama continues with a horrifying discovery: "That night on the way to the kitchen, a woman Jo Jo hadn't seen in jail before filed into line with a slow swagger; blue dress stretched over her immense bulk. Other prisoners clustered around her--retaining the double file, and obeying the SILENCE! rule, but nodding with their heads, & gesturing with their hands in a show of support.--- When Jo Jo's eyes beheld the monster a chill ran down her spine.--She recognized the huge brown woman from the LA clubs where she had a reputation of being a mad dog who would fight anybody for anything.---- In battle her modus operandi was to leap on the enemy without warning, without a yell or squint of an eye, crush them flat on the floor & lay with her full weight on top of them, a razor in one hand, knife in the other pointed at their heads--and a gun to back it up; totally subduing her victim. Bulldozer was a bad bulldagger."

What follows are scenes of women behind bars in which the heat continues to build. "Judith talked to whom she felt like-- yet she too avoided the ratpack of Bulldozer, and Wanda's white cons." Racial tensions simmer. Sexual pairings between some of the women begin, and subsequently jealousies are brought to a boil.

Finally: "Jo Jo had 30 more days left to serve." But she hears some of the lies being told about her behind her back. The tension builds... as Jo Jo's sentence shortens, with freedom in sight. "She could hear metal doors clanging in her dreams. She'd heard them enough." During this time Jo has self reflection. A growling determination to make a better try when released back to society. "Slowly they'd been processed thru the prison machinery. It digested them and was preparing to spit them back out into the free world! Sister Black Woman had played the game right and was going to get out! Less then 2 weeks." Meanwhile, rumors move thru the grapevine. Jealousies & frustrations begin to rage.

The reader's attention will be held captive until they get to the unforgettable-- and unexpected ending of this classic Women's Prison Dike Novel!

JOURNEY:
My Journal. Current, 2007 being the latest installment. The first five books (Lamentations—not individually published--, Infinite Love; Daughters Of Courage--A New Order; Midrash/Commentary; Works) has been bound together and sold as LAMENTATIONS IN THE COOL OF THE EVENING. JOURNEY is now continuing with the sixth book, COMPASSION.

L.

LAMENTATIONS IN THE COOL OF THE EVENING:
Contains the first five books of JOURNEY, which are: Lamentations (not sold individually), INFINITE LOVE, DAUGHTERS OF COURAGE—A NEW ORDER OF JESUS CHRIST, MIDRASH/COMMENTARY, &, WORKS. It is a prophetic book full of poetry, admonitions for the human race to get a grip on itself as we go headlong tumbling scientifically, warlike, thru the computer age on the threshold of stellar space. It speaks to Multi-Faith religion, and in the short section called DAUGHTERS –A NEW ORDER, discusses a monastic Order in which all-faiths which hold God(ess) paramount will live together in simplicity, harmony, sharing, keeping their vow of poverty & to do service.— To go out on social actions to better this tired world. LAMENTATIONS is a minor bible for the New Age.

LAVENDERETTE OF MY SOLITUDE:
A play in 3 acts. 10-plus characters, by Master Author Red Jordan Arobateau is surrealistic, at times speaking thru the mouths of its highly controversial cast in symbolism, yet portrayed in street-level gritty realism. It has a great plot. You can read it like a novel. Characters from the highest to the lowest are assembled Christian Nun Sister Lavenderette, ex-communicated by her church, to the incorrigible street woman, Miss No Penny, too poor to own a pair of shoes that fit. A Jewish Activist-Publisher, and Christ, played as a ragged homeless m2f transsexual, are part of the cast. Master Playwright Red Jordan Arobateau's players are as diverse & fascinating as what they have to say. Here is a quote about Sister Lavenderette, for whom this work (one of a trilogy) is named: this play will be about a nun, Mother Teresa-like. But more worldly, more feminist, and not under the thumb of the Pope of Rome. A kind of free-lance nun. Humorous, action packed and fast moving. There s love; the Gypsy, a witch, & mystic revealed to be a stealth transsexual finds a lover. There is interesting contrast & dialogue
between Red a transsexual f2m man, and Bo a young butch dike, non-transitioned. The Prostitute, Beggar and Miss No Penny a m2f streetwalker of a low degree are humorous as well as thought provoking. This trio provides rich tableaux with their street antics. Their histories unwind thru the eyes of Sister Lavenderette. There is a surrealistic addition of The Murderer who brings a rough awakening to the frail bonds of comfort formed by the others. The introduction and final scenes are set in a place out of time in misty zone in

which the play transcends its characters to probe the mysteries of life itself, thereby rising to a greater intensity. Book Review provided by **RED JORDAN PRESS, 2006**

LAY LADY LAY:
This highly erotic novella by one of the worlds cutting-edge Artist-Writers of Homoerotic Lez/Bi/Trans fiction begins with a clue as to it's content: "San Francisco's got a monster menu. Just a taste whets the imagination. Some who pass thru or hear about it, must go there for a deep drink. We've got the freakish nature of people, plus scum & sleaze here to provide props to make The Scene. And a sophistication to tolerate different lifestyles." LAY LADY LAY has two main characters, The Woman, Nicki, and butch dike Whitey; plus some peripheral people with whom the main players interact-- which adds to their character development-- and the Spice! This story begins when The Woman walks into a lesbian bar: "She had come from a small town near the Oregon border. 32 years old. Blond, full figure; about 5'3", very feminine.-- She had heard about this lesbian bar from another woman downtown where she'd been staying; surviving in & out of a few sleazy hotels when she had the price, and going home with people she met in hustling bars when she didn't." The descriptions of Nicki are extensive: "(She) wore bluejeans tight and designer stitched to fit her sleek curves, a lady jacket with a decorative pin, blouse, ladies' cowboy boots; fluff blond hair to her shoulders with curl; and a hint of makeup. Image she projected was, 'a walk on the wild side.' To whom domestic life was too tame--or too hazardous to her sanity."
Soon a challenge is given, the gauntlet dropped to dykes of the world who would dare rise to the occasion: "In her eye and mind; and within her body, it was a lesbian she wanted. To give a woman first crack at her. If it didn't work out, if the dyke couldn't perform, then she'd take her need elsewhere to be filled. Back downtown where she'd been & make some money too. And was real serious about it. A woman who moved in and out of the fringes of the gay world."
We find out about the big dyke: "Wind moved the white-blond hair of the big woman in a buckskin jacket, as she strode to the entrance of the bar. Thru the open door, scent of Patchouli oil, that of the style of the Hippies & their love beads. Click of her boots went from cement to tile. Dank interior. Heads turn to greet her; dykes holler; "HI WHITEY!" Whitey felt like her whole body, her whole soul was in heat. Felt the toes of her pale body up to the top of her wild blond hair, 180 pounds of her was in animal lust." Our hero is also well portrayed, both visually & inside her mind: "She'd given up the inner city & moved out the poor whites' way-- into shacks way, way out, or into vehicles. Nomads on the land. Whitey had given up on cities. So, in a few days last spring, just before another monstrous summer full of noise and crime & grime, she'd cut all ties; and a sense of freedom had begun for Whitey. Sold all of her furniture and gave the rest away. Cut all ties of personal property. All that was left was-- a large bank account in the thousands. The truck. A few belongings in boxes. Her union card which had expired 8 months past; & some jobs. -- Living in the truck was cheap."

We find out many facts about Whitey, such as her experiences in the massage parlor--as a regular customer. And: "(She) had been to a whore house once. A proper one." As well as raw sex, there is a lot of SM in this book, which makes it popular among leather players.

This book is in heat! The description of lesbian & women's desire will melt your pants right off! There's also plenty of psychological examination: "Her soul was in pain. She'd let music and alcohol fill her for a while. Was broke, but with her looks it was certain someone would buy the rest of her drinks. This was simply a way of life. --Someone would take care of her for a little while-- 'till she couldn't stand it any more." And: "Faces at a bar. They carry their private pain around inside them & their private hell". When our big butch dyke sits at the bar in her buckskin jacket with the fringe-- all up and down her heads turn and Whitey sees ex lovers on parade. Through their hushed conversations we learn more information-- as gossip about her begins to fly: "Oh she looks like a rough character. Wouldn't want to be alone with her in a dark alley." "Whitey's not that bad. It was a bum rap if you ask me. She's pretty mild mannered." "Well that's not what I hear." "She lives alone up in the country in her truck." "Oh Bad News! She snatches women off in a truck!" "I hear she likes straight women. Overtime you see her she has a real straight looking woman." "Probably because all the women here know about her. With her reputation. She can't get a real lesbian, so she has to turn to straight women who don't know her."-- Are these rumors fact or fiction?

Amid the clatter of a bar full of glamorous women, Whitey has flashbacks of past exploits with buddies. And the reader takes a surrealistic view thru the long mirrored wall behind the bar full of liquor bottles, at long haired women laughing, talking & drinking: "And the mirror said; "I am your mirror. I am a reflection of things that have been."

Of course the two connect: "Night passed. Their conversation circled like cats testing the territory. Whitey couldn't tell if she was getting anywhere with the woman; for she wasn't showing anything about what was inside. About what she might like in her life. And soon, the lure of the ocean called. The country. And to bid adieu to city lights. Whitey turned it over in her mind: 'I can stay here and play cat and mouse, wait to see what she'll do-- will she go to the truck with me?-- And stay here and keep buying her drinks so she can get drunk for free; and at the end of the evening I go home alone. Or I can just leave now.' So she rose up in the shoulders, hitched up her jeans, got her buckskin jacket off the barstool & swept change back for the bartender to keep & saw the woman staring at her. "I'm not such a bad guy." Whitey was saying. "Come on spend some time with me. We can drive up to the ocean." And Nicki laughed, swirled her drink, swayed on the barstool, legs spread, tossing her blond hair in time to the music." The two begin the long drive North. Typical of an Arobateau novel, the scenery descriptions are in depth, drawing a picture of the ocean, the wild Pacific coast line: "Wind, ever constant blew down the beach. Wind never lets up, and the sound of it made a low howl."

What follows, including some SM scenes all too real will leave the reader electrified: "And the woman was trying to loose control. She tugged the rope, pumped her hips, and the pain inside her physical body grew. 'I've been hurt

so many times before. Over and over.' "Take your knife, lift it up in your hand." And Whitey did, fingers now in a different kind of fist clutching the hard metal handle wound with plastic strips..." Another potboiler based on the human psychological drama, character study, --& lust! By Master Artist Red Jordan Arobateau.
Book Review provided by RED JORDAN PRESS, 2005.

LEADER OF THE PACK:
"I was on my way somewhere. Wild horses couldn't stop me." So begins LEADER OF THE PACK, #2 book in the series THE OUTLAW CHRONICLES by Master Artist Red Jordan Arobateau. Sometimes surrealistic, a tantalizing drama opens with a snapshot of a hero from the series, handsome Angel: "A young husband, blond Angel took care of their babies. Changed diapers. And at night they snuggled close and they (XXX rated). As a teen, she had been more or less disgusted with life, with the world. Grown up in a square industrial city whose gay life was subterranean--it would not be until age 26 she'd have her first joy, with Pam. (Who she later looses in a tragic spill.) She had lived too long a lone butch roaming a straight landscape of honky tonk bars, Mafia joints catering to freaks, whose star was a female impersonator on stage, while B-girls worked the audience. Real women, warm, naked shoulders, big breasts bouncing under satin; round hips in tight dresses, jangling jewelry." This, as the entire OUTLAW CHRONICLE series has plenty of sex. And a lot of chopper scenes: "The wind in her hair, knees wide, seated on her motorcycle, power throbbing between her legs; air gushing all over them in a bath. Ahead, silver rails and a cement highway plunge into the unknown." The action begins early: "FUCKING LEZZIE QUEER! FUCKING TRANSVESTITE BITCHES!" Feels a shove; Crystal screams. Angel turns around swinging her fist. A man backs up & she misses, he stands, tall, bigger build, outweighing her by 100 pounds. An evil expression on his face. Angel jerks a knife out of its sheath at her side, and swings it back and forth in front of them. He backs off.-- And Angel knows she's got a gun to back up the knife.-- "I should have shot him right there." The big blond exclaims. Soon Angel and her woman receive a visit from an Important Personage; the LEADER OF THE PACK and his/her wife. It's George & Georgenia, the four go out to dinner and 'Georgie' spins tall tales about OUTLAW victories in gang battles of the past against homophobic men, and their rival gang those rotten dikes, The ARYAN AVENGERS. In this novel we take a close up look at OUTLAWS leader: "Daddy George had coal black eyes and coal black hair. A very large he-she; tall and wide also. Georgenia was a large white woman,-- and fat. Near 6'2" herself, and tipped the scales at 400 pounds. Had lots of jewelry, earrings; was a total fem." This book is about Daddy George/Georgenia's personal lives, The Club, and it's happenings. Soon comes the first glimpse of Oils the dike bikers hangout, where more sex ensues: "When they entered the Clubhouse it was dark night. Inside, the walls were painted black, which gave a dungeon like effect. Women, most of them bikers, many simple personalities; and vanilla. Others of a more complex strain. In back many gathered, watching a show."

Descriptions of the immense bulldike and her wife; Queen Georgenia, their 15 room mansion: "The Mansion had a dungeon full of playtoys for SM (George had established this when she saw it was a way to empower dikes & herself) a sewing room with lacy curtains, a weight lifting room. Georgenia had control of the Master Bedroom where they slept. Her things were everywhere. Her sewing room was to one side, and also a huge walk-in closet--which was formerly a 2nd bedroom, --resplendent with 450 pairs of shoes-- to rival Imelda Marcos Queen of the Philippines. Ribbons and bows; and rows, rows, rows, of spike heels, thigh-high boots, sandals and shoes with pointed toes."

Descriptions of The Queen: "Georgenia was a huge woman equal to the size of George, plus very fat, outweighing her by 50 to 100 pounds depending on the state of her dieting which was perpetually in flux." There's plenty in this book. This novel is purportedly about George, the Leader, but it's also a narrative of the other gang members. Learn more about your favorite characters; all familiar to the reader from SATAN'S BEST #1 and THE BLACK BIKER #3 issued in 1997 by MASQUERADE, Inc. Hooker Debbie, the bulldike who pimps her-- Rip, former Roller Derby Queen. Stryker--whose great idea it was for a Bikers Poetry Slam in TRANNY BIKER #8 now with a controversial idea for a most politically incorrect SM scene for Daddy George's X rated Xmas party. Native American Indian Commancho and her showgirl wife Frosty, and many other biker couples the reader already knows.

Arobateau takes on racial issues : "Daddy George took Saundra's orange Afro'd head gingerly between her huge hands, pressed it against her broad chest, and blood that was on the woman face smeared the leather.-- But Saundra wouldn't be pacified. She was going to go home.-- White bikers in the club might not have realized it, but the (race) riots had been right where she lived; and it was grating fiercely on her too.--And she was the same color the rioters were.-- She got up to walk out alone, with shaky steps of her stiletto spike boots."

They go on runs: "Their hair was full of oil from the bikes, and dirt from the road. It was a small run, not like the Memorial Day in summer, and half of the membership,--50 or so showed. --- They'd do Harley Drag Races. It was awesome to see a dike biker go from zero to 80 MPH hour in 2.5 seconds. Had a Tire Drag contest, on which a biker is dragged on a tire behind a cycle;--she eats a lot of dirt. A Slow Driving contest. A Weenie Bite." At their rest stop they horrify the Fairbrook Suburban Mall: "Like Huns come down from the North, sweeping over what remains of civilization, they had come-- overturning garbage receptacles, pissing in the bushes, and making public displays of their lesbian sexuality.-- Kissing and pulling up their tops and wiggling their tits at the straight women."

RED JORDAN PRESS has republished all editions by MASQUERADE, which went out of print. Next comes OUTLAWS! #4. LEADER OF THE PACK illustrates quite a great variety of kinky & unusual sexual practices including some great Diaper Baby (Adult) scenes. But also many glimpses of their domestic life: "Georgenia rocked the behemoth peacefully asleep under the sheets. She was an immense woman, muscles; had done hard labor carrying steel in the yards of long-ago factories. Georgenia's arched eyebrows were plucked, almost invisible without cosmetic pencil; her lipstick was wiped off."

There are touching scenes of Queen G. & her boy-girl pal Selby: "Selby's lean male body was draped over the bar. He wore female undies, pink, under his perfumed suit and lacy shirt. He was a polite sissy of a gentlemanly era. Angular, a male, but an indefensible quality that was so feminine that it transcended his sex. The dignity of a lady was how he carried himself. "I've lived a hard life & I must confess, I've been a mean woman." He was saying to his old friend Georgenia."

Humorous & serious. Full of great dike biker action. Alive with dialogue interactions. A fast moving read. You will just love this wonderful novel, kinky sex scenes & all.

Book Review provided by RED JORDAN PRESS 2005.

LAUGHTER OF THE WITCH:

Inside is a wellspring of magic from where the Red Jordan Arobateau novels get their 'soul',--the poetry! See for yourself! LAUGHTER OF THE WITCH is a sampler of the extensive poetry of Red Jordan. He struggled with poverty and illness through his teens and twenties and in this period of 20 years (1957-1978) wrote approximately 500 poems both short and epic length. This Sampler contains 11 short to medium length works, plus numerous excerpts from 2 epic poems COME TO THE BLACK MARKET, & DEATH FAMILIAR. Now, take a moment and allow yourself to be introduced to the magic!

From LAUGHTER OF THE WITCH

"Follow the jack-o-lantern lights!
Just like tonight,
while you were out drinking in the tavern,
you accidentally put your foot across,
into the main street of the universe.
See how that foreign feeling
is in the lights!
See now, in the distant chaotic scenery
of horizon;
your witch still lies!
She tosses
she turns
she tosses
inside her crazy quilts.
Hearing all your evidence.
As you strut above the sewers,
she's struggling below the sewers of your dreams.

In the horizon
vainly is the witch
trying to reconnect
with her energy.
Flying
and
flying.

Her voice
that you heard
before ending innocence!
That you feared
 in your mother's scream.
In deja vu
before concrete,
                where your patterned feet
soundlessly hammered it."

From A QUESTION OF SURVIVAL

"Tonight came
to the narrow hour of the wolf.
A pacing cat
        comes to sit on your stairwell.
Those hustlers using assumed names
 knock on your doors made of subterfuge.
Boogies laugh, they know, for they can sniff
 yellow in your underpants.
Moses, he points to you.
 Transfuses his blood across the sky
        into your menstrual smear.
Daddy screamed
 "BABY! BABY GIRL!"
 As his corpse went to the soil
You wail
 for you hear the barroom call.
Night's curtain draws disclosing,
 unveils the blue chimney staved sky.
There are pavements, sister. Walk."

From THE AGE OF OM
"Equation is
oceans at keyholes.
Enormous morning funnels
into pink seashells.

Walking across the park
 don't you hear some heads discussing it?

Observe
how the earth desires.

Listen--you can hear
 what the fossils confide,
        (with bi-lingual chants)

66

about the Eurasian procession.
About the doctor of death.

As Sigmund Freud says
"Now you will find it here."
information;

about the age of OM."
Contained in this little sampler are intriguing fragments drawn from that
amazing body of work-- the great poetic engine THE AGE OF OM, and, THE
IRON WOMAN: THE COLLECTED POETRY OF RED JORDAN
AROBATEAU Volumes 1 and 2. It also contains a brief 2 page autobiography
by the author. Poetry Review provided by RED JORDAN PRESS, 2005.

LUCY & MICKEY:
The opening scene to Red Jordan Arobateau's classic Old World Dike Novel is
at a freak show, where young butch Mickey meets her problematic lady-- half
breed, high fem, occasional prostitute; alcoholic Lucy. Mickey, just turned 18,
is fresh out of juvenile detention in New York City, and has skipped town for
Chicago, Illinois. She's starving, can't find legitimate work because of her
dangerous transgendered presentation; and soon she's at this trick freak show-
- doing it for money with a redhead woman, several years older. This story's
set in the late 1950's on Chicago's near north side; Rush street nightlife zone
and alternately, skid row.
So many memories are contained in this book that if you're over 60, you will
remember. The police harassment. Queer bar raids & crazy street scenes. --
Prior to the liberated air of today.
"In the bar life, Mickey & Lucy were Lord & Lady. Back in their own
environment amid this gay wild crowd, wrapped in music they couldn't slow-
dance to; buying drinks for herself & the redhead from their welfare money,
and feeling healing waves--internal vibes pass thru them from being with their
own people again. It was a gay girl/gay boy summer. Shorts. Tans. Gym
shoes.----- Gee! You two look so PERFECT! Where did you meet? Down
here?" A blond guy asks. Mickey gulps-- it's hard to think-- but answers
quickly; "We met in New York. We knew each other there first." Smoke from
cigarettes, chitchat, revolves under the stars of a Van Gogh print. So that's
how the lie of Mickey & Lucy meeting started & circulated around the ever-
changing gay bars for months, when in reality Lucy had seldom been on the
gay Village scene, but had hung out in Washington Square Park with the park
bums, and, in the protection of their company frequented the Lower East Side
cheap-shot brewery & winery halls on the fringes of the Bowery, deeply
enmeshed in the liquid fingers of alcohol---drink. And was down and out and
knew no gay kids at all. "Is she any good in bed?" "She wants it bad--from me.
& me alone." Mickey says coolly, examining her short fingernails. Then
hitches up her pants, thumbs in the belt, and adds, flatly, like she don't care
one way or the other; "I see the begging look in her eyes, and I give it to her."
And combs fingers thru her dark hair. This virile, gallant butch stud, Mickey
Leonardi.

Yes, LUCY & MICKEY is loaded with sex! This is an Old World Dyke novel with all inhibitions stripped away by modern times. So you can read what those dykes were actually doing back then-- it's not just polite guessing games like much of that passed literary genre-- & between us honey, some old gals here at RED JORDAN PRESS remember they were doing Plenty Of It!

Love affairs, love triangles, clashing personalities, survival strategies of these very poorest of American society --well described by Arobateau. Drugs make their nasty intrusion: "Phyllis came gliding into the tavern wearing a short skirt, & white plastic vinyl boots with toes curled up elflike. Mickey is startled, turns to see her as though she was a ghost. Lucy's head snaps around immediately; all smiles & reaches out to touch Phyllis as she does with people she loves. Phyllis endures this touch with gritted teeth; stands there like a shirt on a hanger; spooky, silent. Drugs have taken over her body & possessed her. She hovers, in the way heroin junkies do; it's their chemistry-- dope re-creates their vibes, restructures them with its own metabolism, like a chemist.   "Come by the apartment sometime; you're invited." A cold smile spreads on her face. An underseas junkie. ---Phyllis hovered, feet in plastic boots almost unconnected to the cigarette butt-littered wino floor of rough boards. "We just need some money. We can cop again." Phyllis says sweetly. "I have a foil package." She smiles. "You know what's in it Lucy. Would you like a cut? Huh? Just a little cut, with me---for free? Shall we go in the bathroom? Is it safe here?"

Cops crisscross the scene-- likewise violent queer-hating punks.-- This is from a day before the words 'queer' & 'freak' had been claimed back by gay people & used as a badge of courage & solidarity. Back In The Day when these shouted epitaphs were an overture to beating, rape or murder. Those times-- often glorified now --when gays and anyone not fitting the gender norm were criminalized outcasts. Read about the real thing from Master Author Red Jordan, who, himself was on the scene!

"And time passed. Life was a hard motherfucker riding them down. Low-class dykes-- some go straight. Others are dead. Others are brave, live gay life in the open. So at the 169 Club they would meet again. It was the weekend, after a long unendurable panic of daily days. Braved the dangers of the streets of night to get there. Hustled a beer from a dyke as poor as them."

Near the end of the starving times in Chicago, 8 months into stormy hair-pulling love affair, Mickey finally realizes she needs to find work. This book is raw & real: "(Mickey) Huddles in the brick entranceway. Toes going numb. Wants to put her fist into something.-- Wishes desperately she had a dick like the johns & could take Lucy to undreamed-of heights in bed & out to dinner in nice restaurants; instead of being short in stature & skinny." Naturally, as all of the Arobateau oeuvre, it contains humor.

Some final words the original intent of the author was to use the original cultural spelling of the word 'dike'--not 'dyke'-- as other of his unspellchecked manuscripts, but as this is one of Red's New York Published novels (Richard Kasak's MASQUERADE BOOKS) it probably got turned into the bourgeoisie 'dyke' by an unknowing typist.

You won't be able to stop reading, up to the final words in this Masterpiece-- but be reassured, besides being a fully contained novel which stands on its own, it is the first book of the LUCY & MICKEY TRILOGY --so you can read more about these characters in Part 2, the fem's story, FOR WANT OF THE HORSE THE RIDER WAS LOST, and the denouement, Part 3, COME WITH ME LUCY. Book Review provided by RED JORDAN PRESS, 2005.

LIGHT AT DAWN:
Ruth goes out into life searching for meaning amid the suicidal seas of meaningless... searching for a cause... for a God... Describing a period of actual events circa 1969, RED JORDAN PRESS presents the interesting, somewhat embarrassing LIGHT AT DAWN; a tale of redhead Ruth, the changes she goes thru and her subsequent Christian conversion. Written in 1979 in a month from notes, while still in the white-hot frenzy of religious dogma of my new born-again status after the death of my father. Held together by 26 rusted staples; I have pulled this apart and re-Xeroxed it page by page as part of my Ancient Book restoration series.

LADIES' AUXILIARY OF THE LEFT/CHAMPAGNE, FIRECRACKERS, GUNSHOTS & THE SMOKE FROM THE DEATH FACTORY: My Diary 1967-1977:
Two diary/fiction pieces from the author's youthful starving years, dwelling in a condemned building in the City of St. Francais.
Uneven font, original mis-spellings intact!--An almost exact duplicate of an original manuscript written in the era before computer spellchecks!
Two diary pieces from the author's youthful starving years, dwelling in a condemned building in San Francisco. An excerpt ("I was fisting before Stonewall") appears in Shar Rednours collection Virgin Territory vol. 2.
 Published by Red Jordan Press1998. Revised edition. Original copyright 1977.

THE LOVE LAMENT OF PETER PAIN:
A play. Old collection. In the continuing spirit of archiving all my work; airing out some of my old books; making available to the public with a limited edition all my best, better and regular stuff-- much of it being of historic interest--- and for all those curious about the author's (myself) style of writing and it's evolution; here is presented THE LOVE LAMENT OF PETER PAIN. It is part of my Re-Xeroxing Project. And is a direct reproduction only, nothing in its text has been edited or changed.
Originally created as a story-dialogue typed on onionskin paper in manuscript form circa 1962. A long rambling 'play' occurring in a black South Side Chicago. In 1976 I retyped that manuscript, photocopied & stapled it together in 2 sections for a first published edition. It's impossible to remember how many of these books were printed— 5 sets? Or 7? (A typical quantity my budget could afford.) Not over 10 or 20. Those originals in their blue covers are collector's items. –RJA

M.

THE MAIDS:

A play in 3 acts, 10-plus characters. Red Jordan Arobateau's THE MAIDS (A Tranny Murder Mystery) is a hilarious, thought-provoking, sometimes poignant theatre piece, which moves rapidly from the power-packed opening scene to the grand finale. You will become acquainted with a big handful of characters from the dynamic African American Miss Bossy, leader of the Ladies & Gentlemen s Saturday Afternoon T-Party , who meet in the Main Room of their elite Private Club, to the lowest hired help who cook and serve in the kitchen. The deep dark secret the elite society members share they are all passable Transsexuals. Romance buds between the highbrow and low, crossing class lines the demarcation zone between kitchen and parlor. Particularly fun is the would-be love affair between one M2F and an F2M as they scour pots together in the kitchen. Into the midst of this delicious brew a body (or more!) turns up dead! More then a Whodunit, this is a funny fast moving character study, which speaks about transgender issues, class and the concept of the stealth tranny. All while being humorous, and its players so engaging that they stand out in dramatic history. Book Report provided by RED JORDAN PRESS, 2006

MAN GONE/STARVAX:
Man Gone/Starvax (Book 2) If you liked EMPIRE! You will enjoy Man Gone/Starvax, the succesufo sequel to empire. Unlike some writers hwo fall down on their 2nd book, and arenot able to sustain the itnest, chracters depth and excitement, this book follows right long in the Unity of Utopia Series. Master Author Red Jordan Arobateau has another winner. Look for it on lulu.com and elsewhere on the internet.
Book Review provided by RED JORDAN PRESS, 2007
Man Gone/Starvax is the sequel to EMPIRE! in which transexual man Star1.vax an adoptee into Utopia, the new global state ruled by The Unity, returns back to the wilds to search for his family. The resistance movement of the year 2057, does battle with the corrupt forces of the Unity. Human drama, science fiction wonder, political intrigue, sexual frolics. Another Science Fiction winner by Master Author Red Jordan Arobateau.

TO THE MAN WITH HAT IN HIS HAND, WITH LOVE:
Old collection. … is another blax-exploitation film-going study; memory-drawn from my upbringing on the South Side (African-American ghetto) of segregated Chicago. It's characters originated in a short story, THE TALISMAN, that was written back in Chicago, maybe around 1963, at age 19 or 20. That tale appears in my recent re-collected STORIES FROM THE DANCE OF LIFE Vol. 2. In this, a longer novel, Rudy, his mother Jose, his stepfather Big John reappear, living in their basement apartment; plus the crazy witch-woman restaurateur Carmilinda owner of the Z.E.U.S., who sidelines as Madame Zena, giving prophecies; "YOU GONNA DIE!" –(This hurled at a recalcitrant customer who won't pay his bill.) Names real (which have been redesignated), names invented. Colors, scenes breathed into my soul those long/brief years at high school, in neighborhoods of growing up or passing thru. I cranked it out in my mad art rush of mid-to-late 1970's, building off TALISMAN's familiar notes which reached back further into the

past, needing a mental trigger because the past was rapidly fading. Friends are already having fun reading this Juvenilia Series; tho I don't think these books are as good as my later mature works, nor as gut-wrenching as some earlier, they are entertaining. Wish I had time to read one now, but am too busy Re-Xeroxing & creating my Journal, PASSAGE!

MAN FROM THE BLAX GALAXY:

Old Collection. Born of a baglady, disenfranchised, illiterate. This is his life as he tells it, full of sound and fury—from the back of the bus. The MAN FROM THE BLAX GALAXY sure is interesting. Inside its covers are flashbacks of sights & sounds from the black world I remember--- albeit a watered down version--- of soul street men & the blood-drenched life of African American gangsta dropouts. Complete with all my usual moralizing/sermonizing from those days closer to my religious conversion in '75. It is one of a half dozen Blax Experience novels I churned out, using the current slang spelling of those days —with an X. ---Which entailed going to a lot of blackcentric 3rd rate moves, reading pulp fiction especially Donald Goins & Iceberg Slim, listening to soul music & dancing all 7 nights of the week away at the black, brown & tan disco (which appears as Soulville in my writings). While reprinting this book, within the master copy (a solid sheet of paste-up half pages creating a folio) I found a page interesting to note; —it a second verso; MAN FROM THE BLAX GALAXY PART TWO baring the same copyright—March 1989. On its flip side the words: THUS CONTINUES PART TWO OF THE NOVEL. Must have loved his story so much that I was determined to continue it! — Which never transpired. Like the Man From the Blax Galaxy's own life it wasn't destined to go on…..

One by one that vast penitentiary—the public school system-- was spitting out children. Soon every kid would be a woman or a man. Run across them, the same women and men sitting day after day on porches. Or locked up in a kitchen somewhere wishing they had cigarettes to smoke, but no money. Older folks got welfare, stargazed in taverns; hanging around because they were out of a job. Many would never confess, the mind-blowing fact that they'd never worked more then 2 months in their lives, and had attained age 25 or 30 barely realizing what it felt like to punch a time clock & receive a paycheck. To buy things you wanted. To choose the apartment you wanted to live in.

N.

THE NEARNESS OF YOU/SORROW OF THE MADONNA:

An older dyke, married and living with her two wives, looks back over her life, reflected in the mirror of a gay restaurant on Castro Street; she recalls the past from within the present torture of her soul. A hot and steamy sex sizzler, with religious overtones! Tour the San Francisco lesbian sex clubs, streets, dance halls, and churches.

This long sought after lesbian novel by Master Author Red Jordan Arobateau is now available to the public! Originally contracted by Masquerade Books, Richard Kasak decided to publish COME WITH ME LUCY instead. If you like big reading this 586 page novel, THE NEARNESS OF YOU/SORROW OF

THE MADONNA is for you. Excepts of it have appeared in Karen Tulchinskis fabulous anthology Hot & Bothered. It's a tale of mixed race butch Sonny Zapatta (Puerto Rican/white) and the two loves of her life, two wives, high femmes Foxy & Kitty.

"It all begins and ends with females. Females bringing males into the world, then taking them to the grave.--More of the Sorrow. Females who live all their lives in the shadow of fear. Sonny knew the Devil--he brings tears. All she knew of those weeks in late Autumn of that year approaching Millennium--2000 AD-- was that she had been searching through the streets of San Francisco for herself. Like an archeologist through potsherds and relics and old bones; wounds and grief's and bits & pieces of the past. it was a struggle from sun up to sun down. A dyke a humanbeing, an aging biological female with all her aches and complaints. Walking the SOMA in circles in the fog, with the clock in the modernistic belltower a reminder of the urgency of time."

Subtitle on the cover of this books reads: A Religious Lesbian Novel. It does have some spirituality: "Ultimately it was not the callous nights of sexual passion or SM flogging with black whips (& the cat-of-9-tails of preference)-- but love, shown through their loyalty. Romance, friendship, sex, nasty acts, and beyond this--agape--a gift from God. Love--a gift of pure gold--not to loose this." In this large novel even Mother Teresa makes a appearance. Don't get the wrong idea, it has a lot of hot sizzling sex scenes as well. It's both! There are discussions of her mixed-race status: "Dark brown--curly hair, perpetually tanned skin; could be Italian, or Indian or Greek. 'I can be anything. When I was a kid, each time I ran away from that home I was sent to foster care and raised there for months--as a white. I'm nothing... I'm nothing.."

"The Madonna must have saw her crying. Sitting all alone. Bitterly thinking; 'there must be a way to take care of our needs, I seen too many lesbians crying over their needs. Unmet. "--Because by Her Grace, this woman, Foxy came to brighten up Sonny's dark hours. Sonny one so blue, I love you. The Madonna must have saw her crying inside; underneath the stern face, scuttling down darkened streets at night between her house & the gay bar...." There are the fallen times; her brief affair with Wayne when she is homeless, and sex work at the lowest period of her life. Currently, Sonny works a demanding job as a post office mail handler at the San Francisco postal facility. When suddenly... the angst begins... as she is alternately tiered, fearful, angry & triumphant! & searching-- eternally searching...

Red Jordan Arobateau lifts this novels opening line from Dickens: "it was the best of times and the worst of times," ... and then, continues in True Arobateau Style--- "when Sonny wanted to XXXX so bad she could taste it."

It's a fascinating view on a demimonde of lesbian life, a hustlers life. The world of hard butch dike Sonny Zapatta. Book Review RJP 2005.

O.

OUTLAWS! :
5th in the dike biker series THE OUTLAW CHRONICLES. Transsexual theme. Further adventures of the dike biker gang. A club member absconds

with the treasury. See the five Warlords, Daddy George, Rip, Lou, Royal &
Hawk, in action. Sub plots of romance & fights. The club goes out on its Runs,
fights and battles of today & yesterday are depicted. Lots of raunchy sex.
Cameo features of Angel & Crystal. Published by Red Jordan Press 1998.
The saga continues. Criminal elements threaten the club—from within. There
is a visual realism that catches the reader up in the action & passion. A few
different themes wind thru this large book, a transsexual Warlord (FTM) emerges
from stealth. A new house for the poorer members is set up. A must read for the
OUTLAW CHRONICLE fans!

OUR DYKE HOUSE:
A play in 3 acts, 10-plus characters. Funny, action-filled. Al & her younger
wife Dolly own a huge mansion which is close to forclosure. Ancient butch Al
is having an affair with a young leather femme Trash. The many queer tenants
in the mansion—including the straight ones—and the black transsexual butler-
--rally to Al & Dolly's aid.

P.

PASSAGE:
Is a mature work, begun in 2006; a daily journal interwoven with short
vignettes, poetic ramblings. It can be found sold in it's separate books 1-9.
Aprox. 1,400 pages.
The Journal of Red Jordan Arobateau, PASSAGE, continues where AUTUMN
CHANGES ended. It too is A Transsexual Account. As AUTUMN CHANGES
was more about the hardcore time of transition, PASSAGE picks up in 2005, 7
years after he's begun. It also flashes back into the past. This Journal is both
interesting, & funny.
It provides a equal argument for both sides of the Gender Variant, Vs,. True
Transsexual debate, which is currently raging today; the bathroom wars, &
gender roles with a lot of humor and state of the art political overview: "An
aside note; (as most of female-born news is never important); over the 3 day
queer weekend; Friday being Tranny March; Saturday Dike March; Sunday,
the world famous Gay Pride Day with the largest parade in the world, some 2
million; 4 Trans Masculine men died.
Gender Variant by drug overdose/suicide?
Transman, violently murdered.
Butch dike; vehicular manslaughter.
F2M transman; suicide by hanging."
It is both philosophical and anecdotal: "Amid time, mixing the sediment of
experiences, grew wisdom; and he began to find others like him, so alone, not
the glamorous; but black women in low rent hotel rooms afraid to go out after
dark to assemble; without sex, without the arms of a love, maybe just a few
lesbian books and records to keep them company. These people who
occasionally reach up from a drowning sea and holler "HELP" via a support
group, letter to the editor of some queer newspaper or radio program talk line.
This stirs up my energy once again to recount these desperate events of my

lower class life and how I'd survived, in vain hope it might somehow help others."

The author departs from practically all of his other 45 plus books available to the public by including eight black & white photographs of his fine arts oil paintings. Like AUTUMN CHANGES, this Journal also has also many quotes throughout, fully accredited. It also includes footnotes of explanation of historic gay information not common knowledge today.

Add to this interesting scholarly reading, which is also sexually descriptive, a great dialogue, and glimpses of a wide spectrum of dikes, fags and trans of (of all sexes) from the past & also for the future! As said previously, the Author's great humor is reflected in PASSAGE, such as the tale of Mademoiselle X and the silver tea service set!

Typewritten in the authors original font and not spell checked. A true collectors dream. Food for the troubled souls of our times.

Book Review provided by RED JORDAN PRESS, 2005

Master Author Red Jordan Arobateau has written fiction for over 40 years, he departs from this to create his Journals a semi-fictionalized/factual account of his life, in the Passage volumes.

PASSAGE Volume 9:

#9 is the end of this semi-autobiographical journal of the Master Artist Red Jordan Arobateau. It deals with a variety of current & historical subjects, through a multitude of fascinating characters, interwoven plots, mysteries, poems, and political comments. Fabulous dialogue. Great sex.

PRISONER OF HEARTS:

Old collection. A domestic maid works in the mansions of the wealthy, while worrying about her teenage son's struggle with drugs at home, in the Robert Taylor Projects of Chicago. An interesting fact about PRISONER OF HEARTS; page 41 is the original scene cannibalized later for a descriptive passage in my story/novella HOW RUBY GOT THERE (STORIES FROM THE DANCE OF LIFE VOL. 3) in reference to Ruby's father. So the reader will find those few pages in the two novels identical.

Now, in 2006, remembering back that I'd done a lot of hard work on these books; thus motivation for their recreation in the 'Juvenilia Series.' I did not want them to be lost—though their content seems trivial now, and not as advanced as an AUTUMN CHANGES, STAGE DOOR, or CARNIVALLA. So herein is reproduced by photocopy the exact same text from one of my last remaining copies (2) for all those interested.

I recall creating PRISONER OF HEARTS in my tunneled-out rooms in that condemned building on Eddy Street in San Francisco's Western Addition district back in the late '60's. Like most of my earliest manuscripts it wasn't committed to book form and copyrighted until a decade later; 1976. It was pecked out on my Smith Corona electric typewriter. The idea for PRISONER came from a morphing of a ghetto scene remembered from Chicago, the low-income housing projects called the Robert Taylor Homes which marched down State Street as awful crime-ridden giants— high rises; ghettos in the sky-- and inlaying that with a new environment fresh in my experience, the home of a wealthy lesbian who lived in Pacific Heights met thru the women's movement just bursting on the scene in the late '60's. Thus Mame Shorter the domestic, and her employer, the fastidious Miss Z. came to life on the page.

Of course there is the silly little religious homily at the end, like all those late 1970's works—me just discovering religion and Creator for the first time as an adult. I've left it all in, embarrassing parts and all.

R.

THE RICH/THE POOR IN SPIRIT:

The tale of a lesbian fry cook, her revolutionary lover, a rich heiress and a ghetto prostitute; by Master Artist Red Jordan Arobateau, reissued from his Early Works series. Out of Print for 28 years this Classic Tale has been reissued! The tale of a revolutionary lesbian fry-cook at the Burger Emporium has communistic overtones!

This novel is great fun & Master Author Red Jordan must have had fun writing it-- a unique and varied cast of characters, true to life, compelling. THE RICH/THE POOR IN SPIRIT has a weary, lowpaid fry cook, --attractive femme dike of mixed race heritage-- Shelly, for it's hero. It also stars a rich heiress, a black prostitute, a wild-hair revolutionary radical. And many other fascinating people beside these. It is set in a 1970's fast food joint; downtown San Francisco.

Shelly is a cartoonist in her spare time: "The next morning, after a sweaty, difficult night which left the sheets twisted, her own ghosts had departed. Shelly sat up in her room in the sun, surrounded by illustrations in watercolor. Gay pink, blue, green. Lady Trash was there. The Dog who talked. Betty Boo. Also she had flowers she'd drawn. These are inexpensive pets."

The plot begins to unwind fast as one by one the players make their entrances: "(A customer) had made some off color remark to Shelly: 'DON'T TALK TO ME LIKE THAT BASTAID', I'LL HAVE THE POLICE THROW YOU OUT! PERIOD! YOU KNOW BETTER THEN TO MESS WITH ME, AND I AIN'T SERVIN' YOU NO FOOD, SO GET OUT OF MY LINE!" "NAW WOMAN, DIS' A RESTAURANT AND I WANT A GODDAMN CUP OF COFFEE!" "NOT HERE! NOT IN THIS LINE!" Shelly leaned across the table, her teeth gritted, her hand groping for a hot bucket of deep fish fries to fling at him--in case he might try to jump over the counter and attack!"

Next we meet a young, wild hair woman suspiciously splattered with red paint: "Lisa was a Communist. Her family was well off. Parents & sisters & brothers were all professionals & small business owners with annual incomes into the $40,000 and $50,000 bracket. Lisa had a degree at Stanford University & had held a good pay government job, but, at the age of 27 had renounced this to 'go down among the people'. Lisa's last name was X. A big red X."

The characters develop and take on lives of their own. Reva Fentress: Suddenly Reva's finances fall through the bottom: "Reva's days were frantic. Juggling her expenses--the little money she hustled had to balance out between which bill it was most important to pay. A partial payment there.. a song.. a dance... another excuse.. but the time for excuses runs out fast. When dating the heiress, (Reva) had to resort to picking up the tips off of tables of the expensive restaurant where they'd just dined. Furtively her fingers darting among the Dresden china, and the now-stained hand embroidered Norwegian lace napkins to pick up that $10 bill."

There's racism & reverse racism: "(Allison Cashmore's) Smoky gray eyes stared warily for a moment at this servant who brought her breakfast... The rather gross, dumpy black maid of middleage. Then Allison shoved her plates of eggs away in disdain, stifling a mental shudder; "I wonder if she can tell I'm sleeping with a black lover... they say these blacks have a heightened sense of intuition..... " The idea that Bertha, lugubriously going about her kitchen cleaning might have picked up the truth of their sordid affair by some kind of Unknown Powers-- African Powers--disturbed the Heiress greatly --on one hand, yet.. on the other, gave her an even more sublime pleasure... Erotically charged. A kinky twist! Here she was in the presence of her black servant, while only days ago she'd had one of her kinswomen in bed, underneath her, moaning to the rhythms of their bodies in a tryst of lovemaking!"

See the politics! "As she sped down the freeway, white exhaust from the tailpipe of her sports car was an indicator of gross pollution of indigenous lands of native peoples where oil is pumped up from under their earth-- adding carcinogens, lead, nickel, to surface water used for drinking and bathing. Turning their rivers and wildlife habitats into oozing slime pips of spilled oil.-- Early death to third world people. A poisoned fourth estate land, colonized by American tentacles, reaching, grabbing more, more more.. Allison drove fast, as a bat out of hell--like she was trying to escape the immutable evidence of exploitation which followed. In a trail of inexorable evidence from which she could not separate herself."

Shelly's love affair grows rocky. "Shelly gazed at her lover across the yellow table top. She had chosen, but not wisely or well. Lisa was not giving her the love she needed. Shelly needed radical love, not radical politics."

Even as this magnificent, historic tale thunders down to it's completion, poor Reva, only now begins to suspect the extent of Allison's wealth: "Reva stalked thru the rooms. 'MISS ALLI-SON! That rich bitch's something else! Sho is! Miss Allison is hellfire! She'll take a bullet almost fo' me-- risk goin' to the women's penitentiary!---And she rich! RICHER THEN RICH! Boat... Sailing ships? 2 Mil? Who dis bitch anyhow What kind of Operator is she?"

This novel is complete with the standard Arobateau Political Diatribes & Religious Dogma. (Which ain't half bad!) "Part of the capitalist ethic is competition. And scarcity. The idea that only a very few of us can have joy in this world because there is precious little of it-- so we better fight like dogs over it, tooth & nail. This is a lie. Capitalism is based on a lie. There is enough love to go around. There is enough energy among us to help each other if we would communicate and be honest about our feelings & fears. There could be enough material goods to supply us all if we would share knowledge, technology, resources. If we would practice peace."

Like all of the EARLY WORKS series manufactured by Lulu.com for Red Jordan Press, the back of THE RICH/THE POOR IN SPIRIT contains a NOTES section. Further miscellany fans of this marvelous author might want to know.

Book Report provided by RED JORDAN PRESS, 2005.

ROUGH TRADE:
Short stories. A collection of shorter work by lesbian literary sensation Red Jordan Arobateau. Famous for her unflinching portrayal of lower-class dyke life and love, Arobateau outdoes herself with these tales of butch/femme affairs and unrelenting passions. Unapologetic and distinctly non-homogenized, Rough Trade is a must for all fans of challenging lesbian literature.— Masquerade Book blurb.,1996.
Six short stories. This collection of shorter works is done in a neat spell-checked & edited font. Contains the following titles: Pleasure in the Glitter Gutter, After the Trick Was Turned, Rough Trade; Cum Hard, Do the Slang-Slang, Yes!, Confessions of a Lesbian Trick. The 12 stories in these 2 volumes are full of action, sex, spirituality, humor, race issues, philosophy, violence. They are gritty and realistic. Published by Red Jordan Press 2001--3rd edition. Copyright 1991. From Cum EZ-Lesbian Cum Stories with Feeling & Meaning Vol. 1-5. 320 pages.

S.

SATAN'S BEST:
3rd edition of this classic dike biker novel. SATAN'S BEST is volume #1 in the ten book lesbian biker series THE OUTLAW CHRONICLES. Written in 1993. In this action-packed novel we are introduced to the gang of raunchy and glamorous biker women, including the 5 Warlords who run the Outlaws. Enter beautiful blond butch Angel--lone rider on the storm. If you've read LEADER OF THE PACK, or, THE BLACK BIKER you must read this!

IN THE STRANGE EMBRACE OF A PRODIGAL:
Tale of a super-sensitive street woman who discerns the soul through the facades of life. Her political views. Her encounters with the hard shells of people in San Francisco during the era of the Viet Nam war. Tenderloin & North Beach scenes. An ongoing rambling monologue of one of the world's common saints. Will you be ready for the hard and terrible ending to this book? Copyright 1976. Originally written circa 1968. Review by Red Jordan Press 1998.

STREET OF DREAMS (Gay, Lesbian, Bisexual, Transsexual F*ck Stories Vol. I & 2)
This collection of lez-bi-trans fiction is one of Red Jordan's all time Best Sellers. Used in classes at UC Berkeley, it's the original, unspellchecked document fresh from the pen of a New Man. Author Red reveals the angst & action of early transition's first months on Testosterone. Beginning with his introduction & notes: "The characters (in STREET OF DREAMS) like myself, are struggling with their sexuality; struggling with their economics; struggling with their lives." And: "As of the last 5 months I've been traveling thru the transgendered pipeline as an FTM transsexual." This volume, part of a 2 volume set, contains 6 transsexual tales, and some additional works, the never-before published A LITTLE BIT OF THIS, A LITTLE BIT OF THAT, plus

AT MR. LEE'S, and, Red's world-famous essay-story on race, NOBODY'S PEOPLE.

The first tale, FUCKING BOY PUSSY deals with the arrangement of an FTM (female-to-male) transsexual and a gay boy: "There's enough maleness in her/him to attract the femaleness in him. 'He will probably never be a tranny...' S/he thinks. They sat on the sofa in the moonlight... It had been a long time since s/he'd had sex, and he looked so erotic.... "Come here." S/he said. His face turned from a profile; he looked at Star. "Come here. I want to play with your hair." I had to see if he'd obey orders, that's basic.... He smiled a funny smile and slid the remaining distance over the sofa." We must remind the reader, these certainly are not conventional stories--even for a tranny.

The title piece STREET OF DREAMS is next. Certainly anything but conventional-- including the protagonist's, a homeless FTM's religious views. As the majority of these stories, it involves both 'the girls' and 'the men': "A tell-tale-tall drag queen/pre-op MTF Transsexual fleets thru the street of dreams.-- She, like a butterfly is too beautiful to hesitate here, but must flit about from her room to comparative safety in the Laundromat--in a big hurry on long daintily shaved legs." And: "Long ago the white horse withdrew it's golden tides leaving the nightmarish black web of reality plus its glistening neon cop paranoia watching me in each fang-tooth fiend face. But I made my way here. I came to see God like a lover. Eagerly. I am going to se God like She is my mistress. Going to see God like a virgin for his very first time. Going to see God like the last supper on earth. Like the breath of a dying souls last seconds on this planet."

INTERLUDES (MTF/FTM) is set in a Sex Club in San Francisco: "All the broken hearts are here... Looking.. The cinematopic view of our world-- it's scope of drag pre-ops, bi-genders, queens, broads & bio girls, TV's, transsexuals, new men, lesbians, straights, gays; and assorted freaks of the industry with all their mental baggage. Hung in a vast B&D web of drugs; heroin, crack cocaine."

A LITTLE BIT OF THIS, A LITTLE BIT OF THAT --(The Hermorphadites Theme Song),-- the title of the story adds, in parentheses; but it probably should say, The Bisexuals Theme Song! This is an early work, thrown into the mix. Circa 1966. Written while the author was still living in Chicago under it's harsh Vice Code Laws. A fascinating study of a woman finding herself when she meets 3 outlaw hippie chicks who've hitchhiked cross country from the West Coast.

The next is also a Blast From The Past, AT MR. LEE'S in which we are reintroduced once more to one of Arobateau's fabulous stock characters Mr. Lee-- from WHERE THE WORD IS NO. It is set in a theatrical stage set atmosphere, the artificial construct of a tourist area which has been superimposed upon the former, older community of beatniks/hippies: "Old Town was a part of Chicago where people's mannerisms & dress attempted to match the cravings of their inner identities. It was not like the suburbs where robots live, who dress alike, walk uptight, afraid to be unique.---So everytype of conversation & character was here. Take a stroll down Broadway, a man drag that cuts thru Old Town & turn at Wells street. Go past the sidewalk cafes, the tourist traps-- Originally this was an artist colony, but shop owners

& landlords have exploited it; jacked up prices. It is 1966, and today it swarms with tourists." We are introduced to some fascinating characters male, female/gay straight in this fabulous tale: "Mr. Lees whole life, family, fun & recreation, was wrapped into a single package.-- Tricking. His nightly voyages out into the street to meet a man. Night after night excitement which proved hollow the morning after. On Wall Street the word is business. Here, it's trade.--- From the stoop he eyed a young hustler. The man slowly ambled along pretending to look in shop windows, but his eyes were diamonds & dollarsigns. And Mr. Lee hated to pay for it. It was better by mutual physical need." So much history is jampacked into these older stories, counterbalanced by such a great futuristic vision of the trans work, all done in fine, poetic, action packed writing; it makes this collection a collectors item.

BUDDY'S, a homoerotic FTM on FTM scene in a peep show booth follows: "Suddenly Scott feels a hard familiar touch. A hand clenches his shirt collar at the back of his neck. He's being pushed in an unmistakable direction-- down. Down on his knees to the floor to-----"

SEX LIFE AMONG PERVERTS is the next to last of the trans tales. It involves a broke FTM hustler and a more affluent MTF-- or is 'she' actually a transvestite with an agenda of her own?

NOBODY'S PEOPLE-- Red Jordan's study of mix-race heritage is reprinted here. It is a welcome addition to this volume which spans race, class and gender lines: "New York City. A white woman asks me; "What Nationality are you? Basque?" "Basque?" "It's in the Southern part of France." "No." "Italian?" "No, guess again." "You must have an Indian grandparent." Then she told her. "OH!" Drawing back. "Well! You don't LOOK like it!" Her white face flashes red. Suddenly the relationship between them has changed. The power balance must be readjusted. "OH. That must have been difficult for you, growing up!" (A few say. "Oh, you've had it easy!") Or, "Excuse me!" And they walk away and avoid me like death."

The final story in this Not To be Missed Historic Collection is LOVE & SEX ON THE FRONTLINE: "A transwoman is in distress! She has no where to sleep tonight. A major difficulty. She went to the homeless shelter and wanted to get in the woman's' side.-- Had her make up on, dressed as a woman, and estrogen has softened her body-- but the staff read her as a biological male. She showed her ID, saying female, but they told her she had to get a doctors certificate before they'd let her in the woman's side.-- And it's 3am."

STREET OF DREAMS holds a lot of feminist theory-- as it applies both to biological females and transwomen (new females)-- interlaced through this raw, rough sometimes brutal and highly sexual drama.

STREET OF DREAMS has a companion, labeled Volume 3, DOING IT FOR THE MISTRESS. Read the set and understand more deeply the new phenomenon which is sweeping planet earth-- Transexuality/Transgenderism; those kissing cousins of the gay movement, but who have entirely their own identity. We can't say enough about this book in such a short space. And we have only quoted from the more tame episodes for this book report-- get the real work and see for yourself!

Book Review provided by RED JORDAN PRESS, 2005.

STORIES FROM THE DANCE OF LIFE, VOL. 1:

7 shorter stories by the Master Artist, republished from their first edition in the 1970's: A BUTCH IN LOVE; a newly discovered manuscript never before in print, in which a street dike entertains 2 prostitutes on the steps of a ghetto tenement. CATMAN'S CORNER. Wonderful tale of an odd collection of panhandlers proselytizing on a windswept corner, during the Viet Nam war. JULIE, the strange happenings in a gay tavern on Women's Night. CONFESSIONS OF A NOT-SO-EX-ALCOHOLIC, Red's premiere piece on kicking alcohol 30 years ago. WHITER THEN BLACK, on people of mixed race heritage. MEINE THEORY BY KLARE REIGER--A TRILOGY. This is a longer work about a German emigrant, seamstress, and her unique views, after having survived the shattering experiences of World War Two. And CENTER IN THE STORM. A tale which involves a familiar hero, red head butch Stormy. This collection ends with a NOTES section which discusses some fine points and history about the content.

STORIES FROM THE DANCE OF LIFE, VOL. 2:
7 shorter stories by the Master Artist. Including: THOSE NORTHERN LIGHTS. Two lesbian women spend an evening at the apartment of a strange, alienated man. RESTORATION OF THE LOST, about 'The Missionary Of The Bars', red-head butch Stormy. MY SOUL WAS RED; a lesbian contemplates pregnancy while on a gambling spree in Reno. THE INVISIBLE NIGGER, a ghetto player of mixed race heritage. THE TALISMAN; a glimpse of black South Side Chicago circa 1970's. AT AN EARLY AGE, This is a longer work which takes up about one third of the book--holding the reader spellbound with the accounts of 'Prince', a handsome African American stud's success with ladies so numerous that they spill out of the pages one after another! Plus LA PAN DE LA VIDA, one of Red's Hispanic works. Poignant; about an elderly Mexican grandmother and her Angla doctor. Followed by a NOTES section which is very informative. By RED JORDAN PRESS.

STORIES FROM THE DANCE OF LIFE VOL. 3.
The first two short works in Vol. 3., are autobiographical as the author explains in the NOTES section-- a welcome additional input-- at the collections very end. IT'S SO EASY TO BE A REDNECK portrays the young artist, late 1967, days of the Flower Children; having become homeless, piling up a few belongings in boxes along with his dog, easel, & guitar into his truck and hitting the road. He is given a place to crash for 2 weeks in Marin County -- that bastion of wealth of the privileged class. It is a period piece: "Our lives are trips. I use to resent the hippies of San Francisco saying, 'that trip', or, 'this trip'.--- So lighthearted. I had my ideas. I did my thing. Still trying to overcome, to achieve, out of the old Negro ethic. Work hard. Accomplish. That bit. So the connotation of 'my Trip.' Like it was light-weight, but it had all these season of hell come into play, moving behind me. -- In the diminished sunlight just before the second ice-age, I write this. The world is getting colder. World, prepare!"
This truly is 'a collection from the early years'-- according to Red 's NOTES section, while preparing this final volume of THE DANCE OF LIFE Series for

it's final rewrite, he rediscovered some of the manuscripts in a lost anthology which had slipped down underneath a file cabinet.

The second short work shows the author's fantastic adventures with his dog, told in a surrealistic account in 'ROUND BELDEN CORNER. We learn quite a bit about the author in his sharp, imagery, diary-like prose written when he was a teen: "Had a cup of coffee, planning the first robbery casually, 'till it would fit like the ring on a finger into my plans. To steal. I have to steal. I haven't done it before. Disciplined as a child that it was a sin. But never without as I am now. 17 years old, out in the world. I am literally starving. Two weeks go by with nothing but a sack of potatoes."

Third; the humorous CARDGAMES & INDIANS; 3 African American men lost in their truck in the middle of a Kansas corn field. "Near the swoon of dawn, the little truck had continued among the rural styled backroads, & finally having to admit it was lost, had headed towards a single light--the farm house, where, miles off, it had stopped, anticipating day-- that wild drive of night to seek out Beirut and it's unknown direction having all but vanished. They was lost & needed a navigator, tho they wouldn't admit it. How many times had these three men (adults) run away before? Got started, drunk at 4AM in one of Chicago's taverns, the silver & asphalt city, man-made metropolis, wound-up by alcohol, and left their jobs in the canning factory, plus their wives or girlfriends, their routines, and daily pain, these honchos begun driving thru the network of silver highways off to New York, Or Ohio; California, or Beirut-- of fantasy-- driving their car or truck to death, just to sober up & have to drive back the following day. This time it was Kansas."

The fourth work, poetic & sensual, CHINESE HEROES IN WOMEN'S LIBERATION is the brief synopsis of the life of a young Chinese-American woman, Yung Kan, who breaks with family tradition to attend the university, and take a woman lover. You will love this story and get a glimpse of a radical feminist conference during the second wave of feminism, circa 1970.

Next to last, CONFESSIONS OF A SCHIZOPHRENIC TEENAGE LESBIAN. Again, an autobiographical account, as the NOTES section says: "I look back on my work; little of my books is devoted to the subject of mental illness, which is remarkable, since it has been a major force in my life." --Enough said. You can read the rest for yourself!

The final story, HOW RUBY GOT THERE; this glitzy, fast moving piece races along off the page, fresh from the ho track into the readers mind. RUBY dominates a full half of this book. It has quite a bit more sexual content then the other stories. None of it about Ruby's 'dates' or 'Johns', (barely worthy of mention) but only between her sorry parents in the welfare project where she grows up, and between Ruby & her 'men'.-- Some prefer to call them pimps. Ruby is a character who appears in several of Master Author Arobateau's novels -- BARS ACROSS HEAVEN, and HO STROLL. In this tale we frequent some of the same lowlife dives we've been to before in Red's aforementioned works. We are introduced to a secession of 'managers' including fabulous and crazy hi-yella Reginald: "The next pimp Ruby met didn't even share a car, but came walking up the street--albeit with a mean strut and a pimp cane." More about Reggie: "He was so fine he didn't have to mack. All he had to do was walk into a room and stay long enough for the shy girls to get up their nerve to approach him. He was like a housecat taken in out the alley. Women took him home with them and set him up on pillows at his ease, so they could enjoy him and take him around town and show him off!-- He said: "I can go down to the gutter baby, but not loose my glitter. I got class. Once you got it, you never loose it. It just gets rusty sometimes. It's like learning how to ride a bike, you never forget how. You never loose class. -- Even when you fall. You can be in the gutter, folks look at you and see that class shining thru. Niggas are dying to get what I got. I'm bourgeoisie and don't forget it!" We meet a succession of pimps who try dipping their hand into Ruby's purse, including one hard-nosed Bad Bulldagger whose raw, hard, gritty true-to life portrayal is astounding! --Both in bed and out!

Arobateau does not glorify the Fast Life, al la The Happy Hooker. There are poignant observations of Ruby: "She was being turned into a human trap. One that catches people to use them for all they can get. Somewhere in a part of her brain, or a sector of her heart, the real Ruby --that had begun as a child, was beginning to get harder to find." There's a Moral to this story; Sister Ruby is contrasted with another black sista-- Betty, the same age and from the similar circumstances of poverty: "While scatter-brained Ruby was throwing away her hard hoed dollars right & left on dope, junkfood from the shanty take-out joints, fantastic motel bills and an increasing wardrobe, plus taxis and liquor bills-- the dues of being in The Life-- Betty was steady accumulating her smaller dollars into a big green pile. She knew she better get whilst the gitten' was good." Red Jordan shares some Feminist Theory with his readers: "Ruby was struggling. Fighting for that lean mean green dollar out on the evil streets among cutthroats.--Privately she was struggling--fighting the battle everywoman wages on a male-dominant earth; to take her space in the world! To know her beauty! To realize her power! To grow up into a woman and a full humanbeing."

Arobateau has some good political viewpoints about The Game- which we don't find in Iceberg Slim or Donald Goins who chiefly write from a old fashion sexist point of view. Red's take on the whole affair is piquant: "Prison guards will tell you the pimp is one of the meanest prisoners on the cell block. Dirty double dealing; mean as a woman and a man all rolled into the same body. They combine the bitchy viciousness of a woman on her menstrual rag, combined with brawny muscles & male ruthlessness. Like a cat's mind graphed onto a dawg's body."-- "Pimps are male chauvinists and male chauvinists are afraid of the truth because they are going to hear things they don't want to hear. Like racists, dictators, and all people who gain power only at the benefit of someone else who they must step up on, to get over. Thus, they need someone who they must keep under. By trickery or brutality. Who they must oppress by putting their boot in the persons asscrack. However, time shall unveil what is wrong, and if we continue to struggle facts will become manifest that corrupt ruler don't want to see!"-- Hit's home doesn't it! Ruby certainly is a woman 'buked & scorned' but has her final say in this fast moving tale. You won't want to deny yourself the treat of reading HOW RUBY GOT THERE, and it's unexpected ending that you will never forget! Book Report provided by RED JORDAN PRESS, 2005.

SUZIE-Q, A COLLECTION OF STORIES:

The first in this collection is dedicated to: "Prisoners in maximum security--the jails and institutions of the world. And to the prisoners in minimum-- the world itself. From a sister." It could apply to the entire work; a collection of six shorter stories written in the late 1970's, half of which have been published in other anthologies and distributed world-wide. Here are some excerpts from this often humorous, thought-provoking book.

We begin with THE GRAY PRISONER. 22 chapters about a young Latin butch of mixed race; Puerto Rican & white. We find Vaughn in a period of struggle with pills, uncertain about her future, within a gay life, whose scenes will be familiar to many, a bar in downtown Cincinnati Ohio: "Me and Joey became friends. And (they) say we're such separatists, but we aren't. We were play brother and sister. He being the sister."--Joey liked Vaughn instantly because Vaughn was such a man, with her square shoulders, brown suit and heavy shoes. "Oh! What a man!" He said in a high voice, putting one hand on his hip. "You're such a girl!" Vaughn replied." And: "Vaughn was able to express feelings on the guitar that she wasn't able to think about. Feelings poured out strumming the strings with brown fingers. Rhythm, passion from her soul. Her guitar was a sound that drowned out everything else. Daily in her room she vented her tears, her laughter, in improvised songs. "I'd sat up in the Stage Door the better part of a year; I'd seen the destruction. And was glad to have something in my life to go home to-- my music." Also: "Vaughn was in a terror. Vaughn strode to the closet in a few steps, flung it open. Shoes and suits, pretty as a bouquet of flowers. With stubby fingers she picked up a pair of brown boots. "Is it worth Shorty's life?" And with her two hands she ripped the leather apart at the zipper along the sides of the shoe, white teeth gritted, eyes in squints, grunting. Then tossed the broken boots onto the middle of the floor. Vaughn fingered the material of her best blue suit, then ripped it down from the hanger. "Is this worth ------'s life? Suddenly rage struck her once more, and grabbing the sleeve of the jacket, she ripped it off at the seam, leaving tattered pieces of lining hanging from the body and threads like broken veins. It fell onto the rug besides the boots."

The next, is Red Jordan's well-known piece on the subject of being of mixed-race heritage, NOBODY'S PEOPLE, reprinted in SINISTER WISDOM, 1982, and a decade later in Margaret Busby's fine anthology DAUGHTERS OF AFRICA, 1992. "What race are you? If you don't mind me asking." This question has perused me since before I learned how to talk-- in inferences, facial expressions of curious people who saw me. I am one drop black. Raised black. This is the killer--your culture. What is HOME to a person."

Next comes DYKES OF THE ROAD, a great short Motorcycle tale of love, lust, rich vs. poor, choppers & blackmail. To quote Arobateau: "Her parents had homes all over the world. They owned apartment buildings and private residences in which they might stay two weeks out of a year, one in Mexico, one in Canada, in several countries of Europe, and the United States. Homes complete with a staff of servants tending to them, waiting for their return." And: "She hated what she had to do but it was necessary. Saint walked through the park and through the adjoining streets until night settled all over in a blanket of secrecy. 9pm. She walked high and mighty in her white suit.

Proud. But Saint could stoop low, very low and reach into the gutter with her hands with their imitation gold rings on each finger, -- if she had to."
SUZIE Q was reprinted from its original in 1978, in TRUE TO LIFE ADVENTURE STORIES; Judy Grahn editor; and later reprinted in Don Weise's great anthology of gay black fiction; BLACK LIKE US, 2002. "I told her I was a player from New York, though actually I'm from the Sunset district 30 blocks away. And that my name was Gamine, and she couldn't pronounce it & called me Gamma. Like in Gamma ray. All night long & informed me HER name was Suzie Q. But occasionally she'd slip up and say she was Mildred Johnson. For instance: "My mother told me, Mildred, you..." And ect. With all these lies we told from the get go, we were destined to go far. Even if for no better reason then to see what it bes like."
THE HURT was reprinted in COMMON LIVES/LESBIAN LIVES, Spring of 1984: "The Hermit was not heterosexual any more, she was a dyke-- but more often as most Hermits, she is asexual. Artimis did not become entangled with people, yet, she knew she needed them. Very much so. Her soul was hungry. She belongs to that genre of women hobos who rode boxcars across the USA in the 1930's depression years. Hitchhikers and women world travelers. Except that she stayed in one city and confined her footsteps to Berkeley. There are women who walk and walk and walk for days along oceans. Through cities. Nobody knows their names."
Finally-- PEOPLE WHO HAVE LOST THEIR PLACES, begins with the testimony of a foxy femme: "If I sat down & told you the shit I been through, stuff I done did, it would be a million dollar best seller." Astra in a fur coat crossed her skinny legs & flicked a cigarette in an ashtray. "Yuh got to get 'em right away.-- Really catch the audience the first four lines: LESBIAN KILLS LOVER, CUTS HER HEAD OFF!" Catch their attention......" Said she. "The shit I've survived; 15, 16 years old!" She, and her companion, Native American Topaz, are quite poor: "The two sat at a table in the back. Astra did most of the talking; rattling away non-stop. "I'm gonna get me a glass of hot water." Topaz says. "Oh. Uh, get me a glass of ice water while you're up there, will you!" Asks the fur clad figure in her chair. Up at the bar the dike ordered two glasses of water, then popped her teabag in one. "With customers like that who needs enemies?" The bartender commented as she strode away."
Funny, insightful & real, these action-packed tales span many ethnicity's & genders. You will treasure this addition to your Red Jordan Arobateau Novels.
Book Review provided by RED JORDAN PRESS 2005.

STAGE DOOR:
An epic novel, 1,600 pages, in 4 parts. Sold in 4 separate books. (Review of last book) This is the 4th part and end of the Masterwork STAGE DOOR. It deals directly with Billy's transition, and other plot changes, both romantic, and political, off Stage, in a larger arena --the theater of life. Excerpts of this epic novel appear in ON OUR BACKS the premiere lesbian sex magazine-a piece entitled A HORSY HORSE DREAM. Also the anthology BOTTOMS UP Edited by Diana Cage. And in Larry Bob's HOLY TITCLAMPS, an art 'Zine.
Book Review provided by RED JORDAN PRESS, 2005

Red Jordan Arobateau's piece de resistance! One of the world's greatest books!-And it's totally queer! Meet singer Billy Bradford and Dancer Venus Archer: Venus & Billy are the star-crossed lovers. A black/white couple; tans-butch & high femme. Both 28 years old, and artists, who live in San Francisco—The Empire of the west. Meet their best friends Miss Bunny Knox, also 28, a research science, a high femme of color; and her love the middle-aged Doctor Bernie Rosenfeld; and old world butch dike. With a political agenda. See first hand an incredible cast of characters both good & evil. The wild, blasé, transvestite, queer, gay (and a few straight) cast members of The Show. And a host of homeless street people, crazy artists, political activists, slum lords, rich yuppies, spiky haired punks with blue/green tattoos, plus a dog & birds. You've heard of Le Miserables, Atlas Shrugged, War & Peace?—Well STAGE DOOR IS LONGER—AND QUEERER, AND GOTS MORE STRANGE SEX!!!!!! This is some of Red Jordan's best writing! Political & Spiritual medications! A lot of funny dialogue! A big plot, which unfolds!!!!

STREET FIGHTER:
A dike love story set in the streets of San Francisco circa 1992. Though she was small, she walked tall… "it's like reading a diary—stark and personal." Another Masquerade Books best seller, reprinted in its 3rd edition on Lulu.

T.

TRANNY BIKER:
Eighth in the series THE OUTLAW CHRONICLES
The tale of the transsexual biker Ronny--Comancho & Frostys landlord. His bio high femme leaves him because of his transition & he is so blue. The club participates in their first annual Grand Poetry Reading at the suggestion of Stryker the crazy artist. Runs. Battles. Raunchy female to female sex. Spirituality. Daddy George & Queen Georgenia. Published by Red Jordan Press 1998. Comb bound. 228 pages.
A transsexual novel, 8th in the biker-dike series THE OUTLAW CHRONICLES by Master Author Red Jordan Arobateau, is prefaced by a short-power-packed poem which alludes to the Grand Poetry Slam, slated to transpire in Oils Clubhouse. And soon revs itself into high gear with a description of the Top Surgery of New Man Ronny, one of the OUTLAWS club members. As all of Arobateau's work, as well as personal profiles of vivid characters; believable, raw cutting--edge personal interactions; action packed plots, & truth-telling dialogue, there is wonderful scenic description: "The invisible moon completely round & silver had sat on the airy day sky hung over building tops, lurking in wait-- to make its fantastic appearance--at the crack of night; arose & jumped off the skyline into heaven. He thought about his romantic life of the near-past.--Opened the throttle wide for extra power, in gear, to accelerate and came down to the water to meditate." And: "Stink of the hot dense city. The city lay, beneath the thick soled boots of his feet. His crotch, under jockey shorts, itched. Mr. Packy against his still female genitalia.--The crotch stuffer."

Oils clubhouse isn't far away. We learn a lot about our character as he lopes into the club: "(Ronny) rode his/her motorcycle to Oils entrance and rolled up & parked. --Just an anonymous biker. Ronny was basically a plain, almost dull being. Mostly on the sidelines, and never hoping for fame or glory; just duefully going on his job through life. Amazingly, outside of being a transsexual, nothing about him was spectacular at all. None like a bike which arrived at about the same time; which didn't just slow to a stop and park in front of Oils club, but rolled on through the doorway, the rider a daredevil dike in heavy black gear, leather jacket with chains, chaps, jeans, boots, and studded gloves, waving her motorcycle cap and war whooping, her Hog put, put, put, putting, rolled right in off the cement outside and came to a stop, its front wheel inches from a barstool." More about our protagonist, a New Man: "The interior of Ron's house was macho. --A house with no mirrors, guns everywhere, a pooltable in a spare bedroom-- standard play-- which took up the entire space. Gradually a succession of girlfriends had modified this Spartan scenario, including Caroline who'd been there the longest and done the most."

All the familiar faces make an appearance; Frosty & Commancho, Stella Dallas & Johnny, Poet-Painter Stryker, Saundra, Ebony, & some of the BLACK BIKERS. George (LEADER OF THE PACK) & wife Queen Georgenia. Humorous, they sit around gabbing: "Now these days, the young kids, they're going even further." Kelly says in a low tone. "They're changing their sex.." The old bar owner was 75 years old, and was amazed. "And some old dikes too, I hear." "Watch what you say now, People!" The Leader, Georgie commented, "Er' yer liable to be accused of transphobia!" "WHAT!" they all laughed at this new word, foreign to their ears. "My mother use to tell me about my grandmother having to stand up against Negrophobia;" sez Ross. "Yes, indeed. "My mother told me about it. It was in the early 1900rds they used that word." "Negrophobia! Transphobia! Good Gawd!" Queen Georgenia shivered her immense shoulders and put a painted hand to her powdered cheek. "Good Gawd!"

Between flashbacks to some serious events which have transpired, the club members discuss the new male: "Of course they had come back to the topic-- since it was so new & interesting.-- His transition. "You'll want to have sex with your girlfriend more." Says one dike worriedly, in gruff voice. "I love my girlfriend-- I'll never insist on anything from her-- not even my dinner." Replies the even deeper voice of Ronny."

Then the night at Oils is over, many go home to loneliness: "Stars revolved outside the open door of the club house; a blast of steady cold air blew through; biker dikes gunned up their steely machines and zoomed away in the night.--- Oils front door was padlocked. It's single red light shut off. Nothing but the whine of his motorcycle running down the freeway." Dramatic turn of events in Ronny's life soon surface--much to his sorrow.

Transmen will delight to see some of the same stuff they undergo written right down in this book, & SOFAS (Significant Others, Friends and Admirers of them) will learn Volumes! "He was lonely,-- and horny. More horny-- a lot more hot then he had been as a butch dike with exclusively female hormones racing around his system." There are scenes of FTM meetings, Cycle Runs. At the FTM meetings are discussed some serious issues: "All had heard the moving tragedy of Brandon Teena, a tranny who was raped, then murdered in a small town of his birth in the Midwest in a smoldering climate of hate. The beginning of young Brandon's troubles had been money. An inability to find employment, as did a lot of young trannys who cross dress."

There's naturally quite a bit about the ladies: "Caroline cooks him salmon steaks with green salad and red tomatoes; garlic, oil, vinegar sauce, plus onions, olives & mushrooms. He hears the sound of his dinner exploding the microwave. She's turned it up to High Power. She hands it to him, shields her eyes, slides his salmon steak off the platter onto Ronny's plate. "Here! Be careful it don't explode." She says." & how Ronny is outed to the club before he intended to be: "All 3 femmes were together at the same time.--Alone. And 2 of them mad as wet hens at their no-good husbands. "Ronny is no good. I'm sick of him. He's spent all his money on that surgery 5 years ago, and now he's going to... oh. I can't say it...I'm not suppose to ... but I'm so mad!" "SAY IT, SAY IT! Come on, girl!" Cried Mary and Lady, wide-eyed, and began shaking Caroline by her arms; in their great zeal to enlarge their knowledge. "Well, the no-good bastard is going to change his sex!" "What? "How?" "He's going to the hospital or somewhere, where they give classes on changing women into men." This registered a blank with the two. "He's having a sex change." Caroline says, finally. "Oh." The two girls couldn't comprehend it." This is stuff about survival-- in a transphobic, homophobic society. Stuff about being poor, versus richer gays, & all the good stuff you come to expect from the Red Jordan Arobateau Oeuvre.

Written in 1998 when the Author was straddling the threshold of THE BIG CHANGE, this document is a report, a drama, a tale of comradeship and loyalty among females, & a love story. Not to be missed!

Book Report provided by RED JORDAN PRESS, 2005.

V.

VENGEANCE!:

The classic tale of a prosperous black lesbian drug dealer Mz. LaRue Jones & her dangerous band of Wenchwomen, Flo, Peggy, Stella, & Marcel. And the lives they destroy. Her lovely Asian mistress Jade; the beautiful Go Go dancer Marrionette-- caught in their evil narcotics web; & the forces of good that would come against them-- Blond Butch Ex-Con Nicki. Great dialogue. Set in 1970's. Action, plot, sex, anti-drug rants & much, much more. A rare glimpse of black lesbian street life. This highly entertaining, humorous & adventure-jam-packed novel from the pen of Master Artist Red Jordan Arobateau.

W.

FOR WANT OF THE HORSE THE RIDER WAS LOST:

This rough & raw book portrays Chicago's skid row of the early 60's-- with shades of Nelson Algren's Man With the Golden Arm junkie tale: "They would all be leaving soon. The ghastly colored buildings lit up under a neon flash.

The gas lit two dollar whores in an age of electric lights... They would be leaving in wagons of the vice squad. And then, later, in vans, strapped to stretchers with the bag zipped over their face. And the siren not turned on because there was no hurry." This is the 'Q' document, cornerstone of the LUCY & MICKEY TRILOGY. Not as heavily erotic as the other two volumes (LUCY & MICKEY, and COME WITH ME LUCY) This is Lucy's story. Which takes place in Chicago. Near North side: "Lucy didn't talk much. You wouldn't think she was shy, 'cause she was all over the street, all the time. You saw her in every bar, up and down the dismal green and red lights of skid row, all the night through, 'till 5am, and by day, in the good food places (for skid row) ... it's just then, when you got next to her, she wasn't saying anything, but she had a nice smile."

Arobateau writes this one in a more subjective style then volumes I and III of the trilogy; dream like, analytical, with lots of genius dialogue amid under-sea action in a garish green ambiance of North Clark street swimming with troubled souls. We meet her lover-to-be, the handsome black hair butch (who's name's spelling in 'Lucy's testimony'--- ends in i.--Micki). Even at an young age the Italian stud has some game in her: "Across the street, thru the plate glass window of the Hasty Tasty, one old bitch said, "Well, it ain't the first time they've seen the inside of a paddy wagon." Outside, the wind was howling. The sergeant standing outside the wagon, pushing Lucy up on the metal step with his strong arm. Micki turned to him, as she climbed in, and said, "Do you know Captain Varner?" "Yea." The police replied, coolly. "He's over on the Fourth Precinct." "Well he's my father." Micki looked at the cop. She put her arm through Lucy's. Stood there, pulling her back down off the metal ramp. Cold Chicago wind cut through her close-cropped hair. Her hands dug in her hip pocket and produced an ID baring the same last name. The cops let Micki and Lucy out the back, they walked off into the wind, arm and arm."

Next we meet some familiar characters: "Man I been here for two weeks now. I been worken' man." He was busy flippen' eggs, and taking orders from the waitress across the counter, as he talked. Sweat beaded on his white face, his gap tooth mouth was crooked, and his alcoholic eyes, blue, big. Freddy said, "Say, you know Duke's in town." Lucy posed at the counter, dirty feet in sandals, one crossed across the other. "He is? Where!" ---"You might have thought Duke didn't belong there on lower Clark street, he was too good for that. A good looking brother with a handsome figure, and brains. But it was worse if you looked like you didn't belong, then people expected more of you. And you belonged, had fell down here with all these misfits more then ever. Just because he looked good, all the strippers and hustling ladies was expecting something different of Duke. Well if there was any doubt about it, the years would clear it up. Already his teeth were gone, only the eye tooth at the top. In a few years his jaws were going to sink in on top of the crater and cave in like an old mans. Then the streets would have decided and confirmed for him, where he belonged."

"It was 11pm. Lucy had met Freddy, and now they were going down the dingy cavernous Dearborn street, on their way to meet Duke. They turned into the Barrons club, on West Ontario. A dimly lit house, with cigarette butts littering the floor. Liquor house with a shabby pool table in back. And there was Duke, sitting on the edge of a barstool, talking to a group of half drunk men. Old derelicts and wild young ones."

It takes on racial issues-- politically incorrect or not. "Unless she was really drunk, Lucy was a silent woman. She was built that way. If you asked what race she was, she would say, "I'm part Indian, Irish, Scotch, English and everything else." "Yeah, what kind?" "Sioux." Maybe that's why she was so silent. A honky tonk cigar store Indian. Carved out of the laconic substance of a race of vanishing, stoic people. She was pretty, and only now beginning to lose the appearance of being 19 or 20, to look exactly her age. She'd been aging in this climate, on these grounds; old Indian tenting grounds whose specter, shadow was imprisoned by the real blue-gray walls of American tenements. No wonder a curse was put on the walls of America. It was built into the stone and mixed with poured concrete. Indian ghosts who had been murdered and cheated of their heritage. Maybe the teepee was still in her blood. She would soon begin to lose her looks to age. Age from the bottle. Ninety proof. But not from grief, not from murder as so many of us others. No. She almost enjoyed herself, in a hopeless way."

Plenty of Bukowski-like fights: "All of a sudden, a fight broke out. It was late, and two men were putten' each other on. "ALLRIGHT MAN." said one. "COME-ON OUTSIDE, I'LL WHIP YOU." He said, pulling the other man along towards the door, and the other swinging on him. Lucy's ears were so deafened by the pounding of the liquor inside her, she couldn't barely hear nothing. "SAY MAN! LOOK AT DUKE!" Freddy cried, his eyes big in amazement. His jaw dropping. "Lets go!" Said Lucy. Duke had ran after the two fighting men, down between the tables and the bar with all the lames, the drunks, the retired whores, the rotted prostitutes, the fruit of Clark Street, drunkenly reeling, following, they spilled out of the mouth of the bar to the neon lit sidewalk. "YEA!" Hollered one figure, drunk, but stumbling to grab the other. "YEA!" Screamed the smaller one, wiry, jumping in a hunched shadow, out at the big derelict. The snow had fallen briefly on the pavement, casting bright neon lights back up in reflection to dazzle the eye. The innards of the entire bar was gathered in a ragged circle. Ruined faces, watching, expectantly. Toothless mouths yapping... Taunting." The reader must ask themselves, what other transsexual author is writing this kind of quality fiction today? "Dawn had come up two fisted, ready and raw. There was no fear inside the head of the sun. It was a mechanical thing. Faithfully appearing at the appointed time daily. It had not dregs of sleep to rise from, fight off no nightmarish hold or to adjust to any other peoples change of attitude. It was a blind force. Magnetism. Relativity held it to all it's planets in a companionship."

This novel is the story of a woman-- Lucy Matussomi:--- "Duke. (Moron) Lee, Lucy and Freddy lined up along the counter of a Chinaman's restaurant. Lucy wanted to tell the Chinaman to take a piece of egg that was on his upper lip and wipe it off. She kept picking up her napkin, but she didn't do it. "I'm tellen' you Lucy, you really have changed." The restaurant was a dingy narrow place. Only a counter, stools, and a few tables in the back. Menus of cardboard laminated in plastic covers, bent from many thumbs and fingers manhandling them. The ceiling was high, dusty, with florescent lights. "I have? How." She asked Freddy. "Oh I don't know man, just different." "I think I look better then ever." "Man you've changed." "How man, how have I changed. What do I look to you, better or worse?" "Worse!" "Worse! Worse! Oh, I do not... Duke! Duke! Do I look worse, I don't look worse, I look better! I feel better! I do. I look better, don't I Duke!" "Yeah baby, you look better." Duke said, bobbing in his chair, shoulders and head loose. His tan face was cracked around the eyes--in weathered crows feet. Duke spent most of his life outdoors, hanging out in the parks and streets and doorways of Americas big cities. "Well thanks! I told you I look a lot better!" Lucy said defensively."

Lucy meets danger in many forms. A pretty, mean pimp. A psycopathic speedfreak. A gradually degenerating boyfriend with a violent streak. And, drug dealing Phyllis. Bisexual Lucy: "She got a kick, specially out of being fixed by another broad. She had a momentary feeling of having intercourse with the person that did it. Being satisfied. A freakish feeling of being in somebody else's power, as they stuck the needle down into her skin, and her arm outstretched in the woman's hands."

Book Review provided by RED JORDAN PRESS, 2005

WESTPOINT OF THE UNIVERSE:
Old collection. A drama in the phoneroom: an Irish heroine in an epic-classic, theatrical, biter struggle against poverty and alcohol. A great cast of characters! Funny! Am now preparing a physical copy of my novel WESTPOINT OF THE UNIVERSE; updating its condition for the archives and to distribute. Collected a copy; pulling out old rusty staples that bound the work (which was dividing into 7 parts for the sake of book binding only). The pages have begun to yellow around the edges (photo copy from the 1977). This is part of my re-Zerox project. There is no attempt to rewrite or edit these books at this time. WESTPOINT was written directly from notes onto a master, from it was printed anywhere from 5, or 7 maybe ten, 15 even 20 copies, with probably an uneven amount of copies of each section. In those days I gave the books away; did not have the nerve to ask for money. As usual with a multi-volume title the 1st and 2nd books are all gone, and for many years had a supply of part 3, 4, 5, 6, & 7., which now are dwindling. Will bind the reissued edition in as few parts as can fit in the largest size spine. WESTPOINT is a novel with a story line interspersed with 'interviews' from the fictitious phone room callers. A telemarketing office is the environment in which it is set. This book is the one so many who have spent time in the phone room trade have always vowed to write: "I gotta write a book about this job!" Because it can be so unusual an experience, and such odd characters work in phone rooms—as you will see by opening the following pages! --RJA

WHITE GIRL:
Old collection. WHITE GIRL! (And BOY CENTER) were two forgotten books. WHITE GIRL! never went far but was cannibalized for its section about abuse of a teenager in custody to include in LUCY & MICKEY, my first ever New York Published novel which went worldwide. Here is the reprinted intact, WHITE GIRL!. The heroine, Valerie Angelina (in the text misspelled

as Angelena, a mistake which I didn't realize until now, 30 years later due to modern day computer spell check) was roughly patterned after a woman I knew at the time. As many of the Re-Photocopy Series, under 10 copies were probably made & distributed to the necessary institutions, to R., my collector friend, and this particular individual. She was one of several white women encountered over the years in the queer community who prefer exclusively the company of black people—including lovers, spouses. Often becoming the parent of a mixedrace child. This novel contains many scenes from the few lesbian bars of yesteryear which catered to African-Americans. The original snapshot is by Texas photog Suzie De Young Paul who allowed me to use many of her black & white prints for book covers. I remember using a tape recorder for an interview from the subject, but creating a book with a fantasy story & plot. Incidentally this young woman was another in a string of my 'unrequited love affairs.' Sad to say, chiefly for the reason that I wasn't 'dark complexioned enough' to meet her qualifications.

WHERE THE WORD IS NO:
2006. Fabulous Miss La De Da emerges in this, out of her drab self—Mr. Lee, of the story AT MR. LEE's, from STREET OF DREAMS. This is one of the Masquerade books, reprinted for the 3rd time. Black-centric tale of Fag By Day/Draq Queen By Night, Miss La De Da, a middle aged Queen who enjoys being hustled by young Jessie, an 18-year old. Hot Male Sex! Excerpts from this marvelous Man Novel have appeared in the Derrick's Scott's Anthology, of Black Gay Male writing Best Black Gay Erotica.

*　　*　　*

ABOUT THE AUTHOR:
Red Jordan Arobateau practices spirituality in the Judaic-Christian traditions. He served 25 years as an Atheist. He has lived the vow of semi-poverty for 40-plus years. He is a transsexual man (ftm) born in 1943 in Chicago, Illinois, USA. Now lives/works in San Francisco. Of mixed race heritage; White, Native, Hispanic, African American; age 65. Red is a dedicated artist--also an oil painter--truly a powerful voice for the new millennium. He is hoping for public recognition of his trashy gay-lez-bi-trans works, for which he has had only small acclaim. He has been writing since age 13. Poet. Storyteller. Made a living as Newspaper Deliverer, Office, Clerk, Factory, Telemarketer, Karate Teacher, Post Office, Nurses' Aide, Cashier, Cook, Janitor, Housecleaner. Red is a prolific writer who has documented the GLBT (and straight) communities for 40-plus years. He is a documentarian, who writes with love, humor and great ideas. Read his erotic, adventuresome, thought provoking, dialogue-filled mad cap portrayals of the QUEER and POOR human experience. Red has 9 New York published novels, appears in over 35 anthologies. Many of Red's books are used as part of the curriculum at UC Berkeley and other universities. His complete works are archived at the Bancroft Library, UC Berkeley, an acquisitions library, at the University of California.

www.ingramcontent.com/pod-product-compliance
Lightning Source LLC
Chambersburg PA
CBHW022125280326

41933CB00007B/550